COMPUTERS, VISUALIZATION, AND HISTORY

History, Humanities, and New Technology

Series Editors:
David J. Staley, Heidelberg College,
Dennis A. Trinkle, DePauw University,
Jeffrey G. Barlow, Pacific University

Sponsored by
The American Association for History and Computing

COMPUTERS, VISUALIZATION, AND HISTORY
How New Technology Will Tranform Our Understanding of the Past
David J. Staley

TEACHING HISTORY IN THE DIGITAL CLASSROOM
D. Antonio Cantu and Wilson J. Warren

COMPUTERS, VISUALIZATION, AND HISTORY

HISTORY

How New Technology
Will Transform Our
Understanding of the Past

David J. Staley

M.E. Sharpe
Armonk, New York
London, England

Library of Congress Cataloging-in-Publication Data

Staley, David J., 1963–
    Computers, visualization, and history : how new technology will transform our
understanding of the past / David J. Staley.
        p. cm.
    Includes bibliographical references (p.) and index.
    ISBN 0-7656-1094-9 (cloth: alk. paper) — ISBN 0-7656-1095-7 (pbk.: alk. paper)
    1. Computer graphics. 2. History—Graphic methods. 3. History—Study and teaching.
    4. Historians—Effect of technological innovations on. 5. Visualization. I. Title.

T385 .S688 2003
902′.85′66–dc21

                                                                                        2002026839

Printed in the United States of America

BM (c)   10   9   8   7   6   5   4   3   2
BM (p)   10   9   8   7   6   5   4   3

For Alexa Marie, Adam, and Owen

Contents

List of Figures

Acknowledgments

This book would not have been published without the support and assistance of a number of people. I wish to thank Andrew Gyory, my editor at M.E. Sharpe, who was immediately interested in my book when too many other editors rejected it as being "important, timely, and interesting, perhaps, but not easily fitted into our list." Andrew, himself an historian, has helped to fashion a list into which my book could be fitted. He has the breadth of vision I was seeking in an editor, and his wisdom has been invaluable to me.

In 1997, Jeffrey Barlow, the editor of the *Journal of the Association for History and Computing* (JAHC), appointed me book review editor and charged me with the task of writing a review essay "on some of the classics in the field of history and computing." I complied with his request and soon began composing a regular review column that I called "Digital Historiography." In these essays, in addition to reviewing books, I explored the methodological and philosophical implications of the new technologies for the practice of history, both in terms of how we might "do history" and the types of history we might compose. Jeffrey permitted me the freedom to explore, and that column allowed me to test many of the ideas that appear in this book.

Dennis Trinkle has been indefatigable in his support of this project. When I presented the first rough ideas that would later bloom into this book, Dennis immediately grasped the implications of what I was saying. He invited me to share these ideas in his edited collection *Writing, Teaching and Researching History in the Electronic Age* (M.E. Sharpe, 1998). I later expanded on these ideas at a conference at Michigan State, where Dennis and I met again. That conference paper became an article in JAHC and was later reprinted in the *AHA Perspectives* newsmagazine. Just before that article was to be submitted, doctors discovered a benign but rather large tumor near my brain that required immediate surgery and over two months of recovery. Dennis oversaw the publication of my article while I was convalescing. Dennis also invited me to participate in a panel on digital scholarship in history at the 1999 American Historical Association (AHA) meetings. Those three essays, each of which benefited from Dennis's guidance, formed the building blocks of this book. As I was writing the book, Dennis invited me to DePauw University to present my findings to both the faculty and his students, first in the spring of 1999 and again in 2001. I thank both of those audiences for their attentive comments. I have been most fortunate to have received the support and guidance of Dennis Trinkle, one of the architects of the subfield of history and computing.

For allowing me to share my ideas with them, I must also thank the members of the American Association for History and Computing, and especially Scott Merriman, John Bonnett, and Deborah Anderson.

My students at Heidelberg College, whether they realized it or not, have been instrumental in shaping the ideas presented in this book. I must first thank the dean of the honors program, Jan Younger, who was immediately receptive to the idea of a course on visualization and visual thinking and didn't mind the fact that an historian was proposing the course. Many of the participants in my Visual Thinking seminars were skeptical about visualization as a form of communication, but were nevertheless open-minded and willing to try. Their struggles provided me with much-needed perspective, and I thank them for their efforts. In my history classes, I will often assign a "visual essay" in lieu of a written essay. In one class, students had to compose a concept map. I thank those students in my Introduction to Japan class in the fall of 2001 for their efforts at visual thinking. Some students are more receptive to visual thinking than others, and I must single them out. Lorrie McConaha, while a student of mine at Marietta College, was always interested in exploring visual representations of history; she was the first student I had who submitted a hypertext essay in lieu of a traditional written essay. Long after she graduated from Marietta, Traci Dziatkowicz has continued to be a sounding board for many of my ideas about visualization. More than any of my other students at Heidelberg College, Emily Stammitti has embraced the visual representation of ideas. My thanks to Lorrie, Traci, and Emily for their ideas and inspiration.

Stuart Hobbs read every chapter and offered his usual pointed and insightful comments. The first and second chapters, especially, have been greatly improved as a result of his close reading. Many thanks go to my friend Larry Greenfield, who read several chapters and was always encouraging and supportive. The frank and useful comments of Mary Laur forced me to rethink the introduction. The result is a book that more logically hangs together.

Many thanks to Jack Balcer, who first introduced me to the formal study of art and images. Alan Beyerchen introduced me to the work of Edward Tufte; *The Visual Display of Quantitative Information* was the first book he assigned to me for my Ph.D. general exams—as opposed to a history monograph—which should give some indication of the type of interdisciplinary thinker and farsighted graduate adviser Alan is. It was Alan who introduced me to scientific visualization and computer graphics and to science, technology, and society studies. Alan constantly challenged me to "think outside the box," if only to make me a stronger historian once back in the box. My understanding of technology has been further enhanced by my friend David Cress. An engineer who has read widely in many fields, Dave helped me to look at technology as designers do, forcing me to examine technology from a perspective to which I was unaccustomed. It goes without saying, of course, that none of the above should be held accountable for any errors that remain in this text.

Finally, this book was nurtured by the love and support of my family. To list all the instances of support and encouragement that my wife, Alexa Marie Reck, has provided me would require a separate book. At the very least, she read and commented on several chapters, always helping me to clarify points or to remove unnecessary words. When Alexa was satisfied after reading a chapter, I was satisfied. My son Adam, himself an aspiring writer, helped me through those periods of writer's block with encouraging advice. Adam's love of video games also provided me with a glimpse of the virtual world in which he is so comfortable and into which our narratives of history might soon migrate. My son Owen is still too young to fully appreciate what the publication of this book means, but he "helped Daddy" nevertheless when he amused himself in my office while I was busy scribbling away. I dedicate the final product of these scribblings to them.

COMPUTERS, VISUALIZATION, AND HISTORY

Introduction

When composing the history of the computer, historians should align it with the telescope and the microscope rather than with the printing press, because the real impact of the computer has been as a graphics tool more than as a processor of words. With the appearance of fourth-generation computers in the 1980s, scientific visualizations such as concept maps, geographic information systems, data-rich schematics, three-dimensional information spaces, and virtual reality graphics have become commonplace in our symbolic landscape. In fact, many computer scientists maintain that an increasing percentage of the information in the Information Age is in visual rather than written form. As more and more historians employ computers in their work, will they similarly be drawn to the visualization capacity of the tool? This book explores the methodological and philosophical implications of the use of computer visualizations by historians as a vehicle of scholarly thought and communication; it also speaks to larger issues about the fundamental nature of history and historical representation.

A visualization is any graphic which organizes meaningful information in multidimensional spatial form. Examples of visualizations include maps, diagrams, panoramas, schematics, charts, and time-series graphs. Visualizations are a specific subset of all possible images, in that their purpose is to organize signs representing data and information in two- and three-dimensional form. Prose is a one-dimensional medium, in that the symbols of its sign system (words) unfold in a one-dimensional, sequential line. Visualizations connect symbols in two- and three-dimensional space and can therefore represent more of the multivariate realities of representational and abstract spaces. Much of the analysis in this book will hinge on this distinction.

This difference in dimension does not mean that prose is somehow inferior to visualization, only that the properties of visual displays are conducive to certain types of multivariate, multidimensional representation. Nor does this view imply that visualizations are inferior to prose, as historians often seem to conclude. Visualizations are not illustrations nor do they simply decorate a textual presentation: when well-formed, the visualization is the main carrier of the meaningful information.

This definition of visualization derives from the sciences, which have a long history of representing data in spatial and graphic form. Euclidean geometry, one-point perspective, the coordinate system, tables, schematics, diagrams, map projections, the telescope, and the microscope have extended the scientist's ability to "see" both real and abstract worlds. Visual thinking has long been a part of the scientific enterprise, and digital visualizations should be viewed against this backdrop.

Historians, on the other hand, have long been "word people." An anthropologist investigating our professional habits could not help but to observe our use of words. Historians seek out written records when researching in the archives and write papers about this research to be read at conferences or published as articles and monographs. When teaching, we assign both textbooks and written essays to undergraduates, while in the seminar room, we lead discussions of the secondary literature. The written word is to the historian what the numerical abstraction is to the mathematician. From research to publication to teaching, this textual culture provides the cognitive infrastructure of the discipline of history.

Those historians who use computers today often employ them to maintain this textual culture. Historians use computers to send e-mail for scholarly communication or to locate abstracts and other published sources. Some are beginning to maintain Web sites to alert colleagues to professional meetings and registration materials, while others display their syllabi and insist that students access course materials on-line. Some rely on virtual archives that store digitized documents. Some are beginning to publish their words in electronic form rather than in a traditional print journal. Even those historians who use computers to collate data in databases ultimately publish written words about their findings. As these examples illustrate, despite the apparently revolutionary nature of the tool, most historians use computers conservatively: to laterally transfer textual culture from paper to screen.

Using computers strictly to store, transmit, and retrieve words is akin to using an automobile only to park. In other words, viewing computers in this way is a limited vision of the potential of computers. Rather than word manipulation, artists, engineers, scientists, and mathematicians exploit the visualization capacities of the computer, especially the ability to display both realistic interactive graphics as well as abstract data structures. This book explores how historians might use computer visualization as an alternative to written prose, an alternative medium by which to think about and communicate our understanding of the past. Should historians begin to compose visualizations rather than write articles about the past, then the tool will have facilitated truly revolutionary changes in the discipline of history.

While only a few current historians have displayed any interest in visual applications, future historians, born of a visual culture, may begin to express themselves through this medium as frequently as they might through prose.

Young people are drawn to the noisy and active environment of the screen; by contrast, written words appear slow and cumbersome to them. As these visually oriented young people earn advanced degrees and tenured positions, how long will the profession they maintain continue to value words alone? Will they begin to express their preference for images by constructing virtual reality re-creations, abstract data schematics, and interactive visual displays? Will these historians thus pioneer a "visual culture of history" that coexists with the textual culture? What sort of "history" will emerge if the past is composed visually? How well will "written history" translate into "visual history"? While there is every reason to believe that historians will continue to value words and use digital technology solely as a means of storing textual culture, there is also reason to believe that future historians will value digital visualizations as tools of scholarly inquiry and narrative.

Before arriving at this stage, however, historians will need to learn to trust visual information. Many historians view images as intrinsically inferior to words. In fact, historians often equate "serious history" with "written history." If an account contains charts, diagrams, and pictures, so this typical view goes, the presence of these "graphics" serves only to interrupt and divert attention from the text. Visual displays might be appropriate for the general public, or might occasionally serve as a useful illustration for a text, or might even be a dazzling way to "capture the reader's attention." A professional historian, however, would never dream of creating a visualization in lieu of a written article or monograph. The assumption remains that visual information is subordinate to the "real" and "serious" information conveyed through written prose.

Computers, Visualization, and History challenges this dismissive assumption, asserting instead that visualizations are as useful and rigorous as written prose accounts. When properly composed, visualizations are not thoughtless decorations and are not inferior to written information. Think of a map. The information in a map is presented in spatial form, and yet that information is neither an illustration of a text nor a decorative diversion. One could, of course, translate all the visual information contained in a map into a written prose composition. But clearly, the map is a more appropriate medium for thinking about, organizing, and conveying this geographical information to an audience. As another example, think of the periodic table of the elements. That visualization organizes the elements into an abstract spatial form that allows the chemist to think about and compare the properties of the elements. Both the map and the periodic table are useful tools of thought, inquiry, analysis, and communication; they are not merely illustrations of a written text. Both are appropriate—indeed more appropriate than written prose—for carrying out the intellectual task at hand. In many instances, a visual display appropriately conveys historical information that a written account cannot. Historians creating computer visualizations, then, will need to carefully identify these appropriate moments.

We need look no further than some of our own practices to discover such appropriate moments. While some historians already employ visualizations in their work, the bulk of the profession views these displays as "poor relations" to the "real history" historians believe is written. For example, some historians design museum exhibits or historic preservation projects. Others engage in historical reenactments or use graphical displays to illustrate textual materials. If we were to rescue these preexisting forms of visual display from the background to which we confine them, historians would discover inspiration for the composition of rigorous digital visualizations.

For example, consider the historical visualization in Figure I.1. This diagram of premodern Japan was drawn by the artist Bela Petheo and appears in William McNeill's *The Rise of the West*. The pre–Tokugawa period is depicted as one of chaos. The emperor, nominally the largest figure in the panel, is nevertheless attacked from all sides by pirates and samurai and armed Buddhist monks, suggesting that he holds very little real power. The Jesuits arrive ready to convert, while a samurai helps himself to Western weapons. The villages below are aflame and seem disconnected from the actions swirling above. While a static image, the entire scene appears active and in motion, swirling with chaos.

The Tokugawa period is one of order and calm. The active figures in the first panel are replaced by figures whose poses are relatively still. In fact, gesture and body language—the rough handling of the emperor, the outstretched hand of the shogun, the decorum of the samurai—convey meaningful dimensions of information in both panels of this image. In the second panel, the shogun is the largest figure; the emperor, although seated in a dignified pose, is severely reduced in size and is faded, emphasizing his diminished status. The samurai are well-heeled, standing erect and dignified, as if adhering to the bushido ethical code. Note the decorum of these figures as opposed to the greedy samurai in the previous panel. This revived warrior ethic is balanced by an artistic culture that flourishes in the towns, as symbolized by the pottery maker and the geisha performing the tea ceremony. The villages appear more tranquil and, unlike in the previous panel, are now linked to the towns, presumably through trade. The villages are also linked to the samurai through something like a security arrangement. The Jesuits have been banished by the shogun, the gesture of his outstretched hand denying entry to any more foreigners.

Writing out this depiction of the structure of Japanese society linearizes a two-dimensional image. Note how the visualization allows one to perceive simultaneously the whole and the individual parts, in a manner reminiscent of a map or the periodic table. Like these other visualizations, Petheo's diagram is not simply an illustration designed to break up or enliven written text: it can stand alone as a vehicle of historical thought and scholarly communication.

Imagine this multivariate visualization in a digital environment. We could treat the two panels of the image as the beginning and end of a "film" or

Figure I.1 **Diagram of Japan, 1500–1650.** In addition to information about costume, architecture, and other forms of material culture, the figures in the diagram convey meaningful information through gesture and body language, the shading of the figures, their relative sizes, and their location in the diagram.

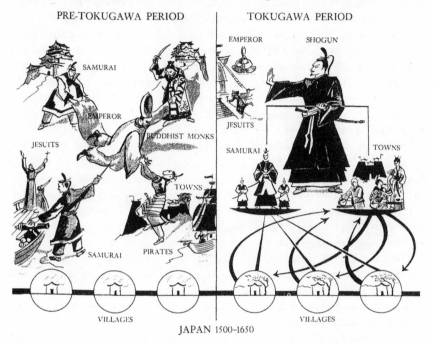

JAPAN 1500–1650

Source: William McNeill, *The Rise of the West: A History of the Human Community* (Chicago: University of Chicago Press, 1963), 648. Copyright 1963 by the University of Chicago. Reprinted with permission.

animated piece, thereby witnessing change through time. In a computer environment, we could start the animation with the first scene, watching the emperor struggle to maintain power while being attacked from all sides. Flames erupt from the villages below. Eventually, a figure emerges from among the chaos: the shogun, who grows larger and larger as the scene unfolds. The motion of the image would reflect the chaos of the period; as the figure of the shogun grows, the motion calms, the flames are extinguished, and we arrive at the final state as depicted in the second panel.

Drawing this diagram in a computer environment would also allow us to depict these figures in a three-dimensional space, instead of the flat two-dimensional space of the paper diagram. In the same way that the size and shading of the figures determine their importance, their relative locations in a three-dimensional space would also carry important information. In this diagram, figures in the center are more important than figures at the edges. In a three-dimensional environment, figures in the foreground could be understood as more significant than figures in the background; the emperor in the first panel could be placed further in the background in the first image and tucked neatly into an upper corner in the second, emphasizing his secondary role. In such a computer environment, we would be able to rotate the space to observe it from many angles; how does the structure of Japanese society appear, we might ask, when we view it from the perspective of those in the background of the society? Each rotation of view would offer a new perspective—and, thus, new interpretation—of the data. This added dimension is not for decorative effect; each new dimension—shading, size, location in three-dimensional space—is meant to convey a meaningful level of information, to facilitate insight and understanding of the information.

This three-dimensional model could also be expanded into a virtual reality environment. One could then "enter into" the diagram, to observe the data from the inside, offering yet another vantage point from which to observe and interpret the data. Pioneers in virtual reality graphics talk of "experiencing" abstract data not as a form of entertainment but as a tool of inquiry and analysis. In such a virtual space, an historian could design an historical interpretation intended to be "experienced" by other historians.

The resulting three-dimensional visualization would be a secondary source, structurally similar to a written article or monograph. A written account of premodern Japanese society would be a "word model": a simplified representation of a complex phenomenon designed to gain understanding of that phenomenon. A three-dimensional abstract visualization would be another type of model, one that similarly seeks understanding of a complex phenomenon by representing it. The visualization would be the end result of the research and analysis of primary sources, only rather than "writing up" the results the historian would "draw up" the results in visual form. *Computers, Visualization, and History* imagines a scenario in which historians employ visualizations as vehicles for scholarly communication in lieu of traditional journal articles and monographs.

Some historians might claim that even if we were to develop the visual habits of mind necessary to treat a visualization with the same weight as a prose composition, most historians would certainly be put off by the technical requirements. While historians could certainly be trained in the techniques needed to create digital visualizations, and while it is conceivable that visualization software will become increasingly user-friendly, such technical skills are not required. Instead, historians creating visualizations could serve as the "director" of the project. Like a film director, the historian creating a visualization—while perhaps conversant with the technical skills— would not necessarily be called upon to carry out all the technical requirements needed to create the visualization. The director provides the overall vision of the film: the cinematographers, editors, grips, best boys, and production crew attend to the technical details. Similarly, historians creating visualizations would design the overall vision, expressed in storyboards and other drawings, which would then be executed by technical staff. Architecture carries the name of the architect, even though the building is constructed by others. A visualization might be built by technicians, but would carry the name of its designer, the historian. If this still seems untoward—historians work alone, after all, not as a member of a team—consider the creation of this book: I designed the words and the overall structure of the project, but the book was built by editors and production staff. Thus, rather than technical skill, historians need only possess a facility with visual thinking to create visualizations.

Even if we were to satisfactorily address concerns over technical competence, historians interested in using computer visualizations would need to overcome professional institutional inertia before their creations would be recognized as "serious history." Professional historians have long equated serious history with written history. We believe that only written prose can accurately capture the past. Marshall McLuhan and other communication theorists have maintained that the medium of communication shapes the cultural forms of a society. Chapter 1 (Prose and History) explores this macrocultural effect on a much smaller scale, that is, on the microculture of the discipline of history. This chapter, a careful examination of the role of writing in shaping our narratives of the past, demonstrates that there is nothing natural or axiomatic about writing as an idiom of communication in history. Writing about the past is, rather, a choice historians have made, an "information design decision." Humans have devised many ways to convey thought and describe reality, through drawings, sculptures, dance, and musical compositions. Each choice reflects a design decision: how to give form and shape to ideas. Historians nearly always choose writing as their medium of scholarly communication.

That choice has consequences for how we understand the past, because the idiom we use to communicate shapes our thoughts like a template. This chapter breaks down written prose into its constituent elements of words and syntax, observing that syntax is one-dimensional and sequential, meaning that written language is an idiom that arranges words in linear order. Therefore, the decision to represent the past in linear sequential form has consequences for how we understand the past, for that idiom shapes the past into linear and sequential form. What changes would occur to our understanding of the past were we to shift to a medium of thought that featured a two- or three-dimensional syntax?

Chapter 2 (Visualization As an Alternative to Prose) suggests just such an alternative medium for historical narrative. This chapter introduces a formal definition for visualization: the organization of meaningful information in two- or three-dimensional spatial form intended to further a systematic inquiry. Further, a visualization stands on its own as the primary carrier of the information, not simply as a supplement or illustration to a written account. In fact, in a well-formed visualization, prose is the supplement to the image.

A visualization, then, is not just any image but a specific type of image that organizes and presents meaningful information, a type of "cognitive art."

In the same way the previous chapter breaks down writing into words and syntax, this chapter similarly breaks down visualizations into their component elements of symbols and syntax, with special attention paid to properties of visual syntax. Visual syntax is not linear; symbols can be arranged in more than one dimension, allowing a visualization to convey the simultaneity and whole/part relationships linearized with writing. In so examining visual syntax, we will explore the properties of visualization that make it a useful conductor of meaningful information.

We will be especially careful to note the requirements for a well-formed visualization. Among these requirements, a visualization should be dense with data, not decoration. It should draw attention to the information, not serve merely as an eye-catching display used to break up blocks of text. In a well-formed visualization, the image is the meaningful information. Carefully distinguishing between aesthetics and utility in the composition of a visualization, we will demonstrate that a visualization is aesthetically pleasing not when it is eye-catching but when it is useful, when it presents the data in a well-formed manner.

The chapter concludes by sketching out the formal characteristics of "visual history" that are distinct from "written history." The point here is not to argue that visualizations will yield a superior form of history that will supplant written history. My contention is that the two narrative forms of history will coexist with each other, one form simply an alternative form of serious historical narrative.

These alternative forms of narrative already exist in our discipline; however, we tend to relegate them to the background of our discipline. Chapter 3 (Visual Secondary Sources) seeks to reverse the figure/ground relationship between written and visual narratives of history. Since we tend to accord visual displays supplemental status or view them as "not serious" history, historians tend not to notice the utilitarian properties of visualizations as vehicles for scholarly communication. This chapter argues that a well-formed visual display is a type of secondary source.

A primary source is an abstraction and compression of actual experience from which historians try to reconstruct the past. The final product of that reconstruction is a secondary source, which is the meaningful arrangement of primary sources. Historians usually juxtapose and arrange sources in written form, but, as this chapter demonstrates, the same tactic of juxtaposition and arrangement can be carried out in visual form as well. Understanding the formal properties of a secondary source will allow us to more easily examine the value of a visual secondary source.

The rest of the chapter details specific types of visual secondary sources and how we might use them as legitimate forms of scholarly communication.

These include historical reconstructions, films, historical reenactments, diagrams, and maps. In a formal sense, these are visual secondary sources since they are arrangements of primary source information. Our profession considers these forms of visual secondary sources appropriate for the general public perhaps, or as a supplement to a written account, but not as legitimate forms of scholarly communication. This chapter argues that these forms can serve as models for how our profession might compose visual narratives in digital form.

Chapter 4 (Virtual Reality) examines one of these types of computer-aided visual narratives. Virtual reality refers to a family of realistic graphics displays in which a viewer is immersed in and can interact with digitally rendered objects. Like an historical reenactment, a virtual reality display in history would be a space where a viewer could interact with objects and people in the past.

Historians could use this technology to create models and simulations. All historians create models, which we may define as a simplified representation of some complex system that allows us to better understand that larger system. Rather than creating word models, historians might choose to create visual virtual reality models. By allowing viewers to actively participate in a model, the historian would also create a simulation. Unlike a model, which is unaffected by viewer choice, a simulation unfolds as a result of the decisions of a viewer, something like a visual hypertext. In designing virtual reality spaces which permit viewers choice over the direction of the visual narrative, historians would need to become more conversant with alternative scenarios in the past, what we usually term counterfactuals. The technology would therefore suggest new ways to think about the narrative of the past. The chapter includes examples of some early efforts at representing the past in virtual reality form.

Viewers of history in this narrative environment would need to use the technology with great caution, however. A virtual reality re-creation is a secondary source, meaning it is an arrangement and juxtaposition of primary sources, a model created by an historian. Because of the apparent verisimilitude of the display, uninitiated viewers will have to be instructed that "this is not the past." Like any secondary source, a virtual reality display is a constructed artifact and thus does not make the past "come to life."

While such displays will be extremely popular with a general public that already looks to motion pictures for its narratives of the past, they might also become popular with professional historians. Instead of writing an article to offer an interpretation of some event or circumstance in the past, an historian might instead choose to present her findings in the form of a virtual reality display. Other historians might then enter the digital space and "experience" the interpretation. Realistic visualizations will change the discipline of history only when they are used as forms of scholarly communication, when the profession recognizes a virtual display as "serious history."

Chapter 5 (History Takes Shape) examines visual secondary sources constructed as an arrangement of visual symbols into an abstract shape, not as a sequential line of words. Long before humans began to write, they created visual shapes to represent ideas. We see aspects of this ancient skill whenever we see a diagram or chart or other visual schematic, but the skill dates back at least as far as the time when humans made the first Venus figurines or started decorating cloth to convey abstract concepts of status, power, or memory. Historians might begin to use the computer to tap into this ancient skill and begin to think about the past as an abstract shape.

If a representational visualization—like a virtual reality display—is a picture of a real space with real objects, then an abstract visualization is a "picture of a concept." An abstract visualization arranges words, symbols, or numbers in an abstract space in order to give shape to ideas and concepts. This chapter explores such digitally rendered shapes of ideas, such as geographic information system maps and two- and three-dimensional concept maps. The chapter also discusses how historians could create virtual reality representations of abstract visualizations, which would allow a viewer to "climb inside" and explore a data space, suggesting a new way to "understand" abstract data. Historians might also use stereolithography, a technology that "carves" abstract data into material form. The result is something like a "data sculpture." Again, this chapter includes examples of how other disciplines have sought to represent abstract concepts through digital visualizations. Like the displays noted in Chapter 4, these abstract visualizations will become "serious history" only when the profession accepts them as legitimate vehicles of scholarly thought and communication.

Historians have written history for some time. Despite the allure of computer visualizations, we might find it difficult to break this institutional habit. The computer may never entice us to consider another medium other than prose. There is every reason to believe, therefore, that maintenance of textual culture is the most reasonable outlook for the future of history and computing. Quantitative historians once claimed that the enormous data storage and calculation capacities of the computer would render all other types of source material obsolete and that the only "true history" would be numerically based history. Those predictions never came to pass, for historians continue to remain more committed to words than to numbers. Based on this experience, I will not claim that visually based history is inevitable.

My vision is more modest: that historians might find a prominent place for visualization in our discipline, that the profession will alter its practices and standards to accommodate a visualization as "serious history," and that the profession will learn to balance prose and visualization. Visualizations will not supplant written accounts, but neither will they simply supplement those accounts. Visualizations will be a different type of medium through which historians will organize their thoughts about the past and communicate those thoughts to the rest of the profession. Technology will have enabled dramatic change in history when the discipline bends to accommodate these new idiomatic forms.

Chapter One

Prose and History

In an 1830 essay, Thomas Carlyle described the problems of writing about linear causation in history:

> The most gifted man can observe, still more can record, only the *series* of his own impressions; his observation, therefore . . . must be *successive*, while the things done were often *simultaneous*; the things done were not in a series, but in a group. It is not in acted, as it is in written History: actual events are nowise so simply related to each other as parent and offspring are; every single event is the offspring not of one, but of all other events, prior or contemporaneous, and will in its turn combine with all others to give birth to new: it is an ever-living, ever-working Chaos of Being, wherein shape after shape bodies itself forth from innumerable elements. And this Chaos . . . is what the historian will depict, and scientifically gauge, we may say, by threading it with single lines of a few els in length! For as all Action is, by nature, to be figured as extended in breadth and in depth, as well as in length . . . so all Narrative is, by its very nature, of only one dimension; only travels forward towards one, or towards successive points; Narrative is *linear*, Action is *solid*.[1]

Carlyle is arguing here something that seems intuitive and common sensical: that events and actions are complex and simultaneous and do not line up in a convenient sequential order. What might seem less intuitive, especially for historians, is the idea that part of the problem in capturing this complex "Chaos" of activity is the medium of prose itself.

Indeed, Carlyle seems trapped by his medium of thought. It does not occur to him to think of narrative in history in a form other than writing. He understands that writing is sequential and that using prose to try to depict the "Chaos of Being" is like trying to envelop a sphere by wrapping a long string around it. He understands that writing is a one-dimensional medium, while the events he wishes to describe are multidimensional. It does not seem to occur to Carlyle, however, that he might use a different idiom, one more conducive to capturing multidimensionality.

Carlyle is an exception, since few historians are ever so self-reflexive as to think deeply about the limitations of prose. Even fewer think about alternative forms of expression. Given all the idioms of communication humans have invented, why do historians choose to write? Why do we value writing over all other symbolic forms? As a rule, historians rarely examine the role of the idiom in our way of thinking. In the few instances when we do inquire about the relationship between writing and history, we tend to ask questions like "What is the best way to write?" or "What should we write about?" Only a very few ask "What are the effects of writing on history?" or the even more radical question "Should we write at all?" Historians exploring the impact of film on our discipline have asked the latter question; historians working with computers may well ask the very same question.

Every time historians write a word or sentence, we make an information design decision. I define "information design" as the decision to employ one idiom of thought over another, one technology of communication over another. With all the data about the past swimming around us, we could make the decision to paint our interpretation of the past or compose an epic poem, yet we choose instead to write prose. Why is this so? For most historians, this is not a conscious choice: it is an unspoken convention that all historians communicate to other historians through written words.

The written word, the central idiom of communication in the practice of history, surrounds us like an atmosphere. Perhaps because of its ubiquity, however, we rarely notice writing's effects on our discipline, how it shapes our thoughts, interpretations, and assumptions. As Carlyle understood, many of the decisions we make about narrative sequence depend upon the limitations imposed on our thinking by the written word. Since we choose to write, what do we gain from this decision, and, more importantly, what might we be giving up should we choose a new idiom of thought?

An Unexamined Historiography

Traditionally, when historians do discuss writing in history, they refer to stylistic concerns. Professors usually hand students copies of Strunk and White or Kate Turabian once they enter a class. These books detail the mechanics of proper style for composing historical works. They counsel students to avoid use of the passive voice, for example, and to cite authorities properly and to paraphrase without plagiarizing. Rarely, if ever in these style manuals do the authors consider deeper theoretical issues about the cognitive role writing plays in our discipline. In this case, "writing and history" is a matter of style: how to write well.

If historians do think about writing at a level beyond compositional mechanics, it is in relation to the content of the words. Articles dealing with "writing and history" tend to discuss issues of interpretation and perspective, such as "writing about postcolonialism" or "writing about the Cold War." Writing here refers to the "literature of a field," those writings that identify the boundaries of debate surrounding a given topic. More generally, historians might debate the proper subject matter of history. A current debate surrounds social history versus political history. Should we write about the powerless or only the elites with power? Like the above example, those who write on the issue of writing and history from this perspective are not self-reflexively examining the idiom of communication. As in the above case, the medium is a given: "writing and history" refers to what we write.

Philosophers of history influenced by literary criticism have called attention to the "given" status of the written word in history. Historians such as Hayden White have examined how the medium of writing influences the shape of an historical narrative. White concludes in his book *Metahistory* that the medium of the written word is not a passive conduit of information. How an historian writes influences the past that he reconstructs. White's concerns are not merely stylistic; that is, he is not concerned with compositional style alone. Rather, he is interested in how the written form shapes historical content.

White reminds historians that history is codified in "historical works." He defines an historical work as "a verbal structure in the form of a narrative prose discourse that purports to be a model, or icon, of past structures and processes in the interest of *explaining what they were by representing* them."[2] Once they are emptied of their content, these historical works are revealed to have a formal structure that can be analyzed. Having carried out this exposure of the formal structure, White observes that these secondary sources have a "deep structure," a conceptual apparatus that shapes the resulting narrative. Each work of history is made up of "modes of discourse." White identifies three such modes. The "mode of emplotment" refers to the type of plot devices an historian might use to give meaning to a story. The "mode of argument" refers to the formal, explicit, or discursive rhetorical strategies used by an historian. The "mode of ideological implication" refers to the ethical stance taken by the author.[3] By examining the structural properties of the works of nineteenth-century historians such as Hegel, Ranke, and Burckhardt, White concludes that the deep verbal structure of their writings shaped their interpretations. The implications are significant; they suggest that given the same "facts" about the past, an historian's linguistic choices may result in different accounts of that past. In other words, writing is not a passive conduit. A written work of history is an abstraction, a reconstruction of the past, which should not be confused with the past itself.

One of the implications arising from White's book and from the works of postmodern linguistic theorists generally is that since the medium influences the resulting narrative, experimenting with the structural form should affect the content. The journal *Rethinking History,* for example, is devoted to exploring the theoretical questions that arise from such experiments with form. One of the journal's editors, Robert Rosenstone, echoing the thoughts of White, argues that we should look to the experimental forms of literature produced in the twentieth century for models of composition in history. Historians should take this step not simply for stylistic reasons, but to seek new forms of historical representation by experimenting with the idiom, the conduit of thought.[4]

When an historical work is so deconstructed as to reveal its underlying formal structure, we can then gain a clearer appreciation of the role of the medium of writing in the construction of historical narrative. That structure at its heart, according to White, is a verbal structure. The philosopher of history Michael Stanford has similarly laid bare the underlying structures of historical thought. For Stanford, "history, like poetry and song, is a way of using language." After pulling away the symbolic layers of an historical work, we are left with its irreducible core: history is inexorably bound to language. "Whether spoken or written," argues Stanford, the structure of an historical work "is a construction in words."[5]

As important as White's book is to our understanding of how structural form shapes content, few historians have jumped to the next level of analysis and asked the question "Why do we write at all?" That is, could some other medium besides words and writing lie at the core of an historical work? Must the structure of an historical work be written and verbal, or could it be something else, say visual and spatial? In each of the above cases (White, Rosenstone, Stanford), after all the literary deconstruction and structural analysis, the written word remains a given, the axiomatic first principle of historical thought. Historians will not be able to think about the visualization of history in digital form until they carefully rethink this axiomatic core of our discipline.

Historians who study the effects of film on the discipline of history represent one group who have reexamined this axiomatic core. White, again, has been at the forefront of these discussions. He coined the term "historiophoty," which he defined as "the representation of history and our thought about it in visual images and filmic discourse." If a written history is a constructed artifact, argued White, what prevents historians from constructing the past through some other medium, say film images? "Every written history," he wrote, "is a product of processes of condensation, displacement, symbolization, and qualification exactly like those used in the production of a filmed representation. It is only the medium that differs, not in the way the messages are produced."[6]

That medium does affect the message. Rosenstone, especially, is interested in how the medium of film shapes the message of history. Film is especially well-suited to depicting information difficult to convey through words alone, such as landscape, scene, atmosphere, and the actions of crowds or soldiers in battle. Unlike most historians who critique film as a medium of historical thought, Rosenstone is less concerned with issues of interpretation, that is, whether a film account is as accurate as a written account. Instead, Rosenstone is interested in how film techniques and conventions produce an alternative narrative structure of the past and how those conventions compare to written history. Note that neither White nor Rosenstone is arguing simply for the use of visual evidence to supplement a written account; they are arguing for, in effect, visual history as a type of secondary source.[7]

Rosenstone, White, and Stanford have forced historians to look carefully at how we communicate. They also suggest that we think about why we communicate as we do. White and Rosenstone—and very few others—dare to ask "should we communicate through some other medium?" This is a question most historians do not ask, for we take it as axiomatic—even as an expression of faith—that proper history shall be written.

History is written, it seems, because we say it is. Further, we look to the past for justifications of this choice. Like most historians, Hegel finds the roots of our discipline among the ancient Greeks. Herodotus and Thucydides "simply transferred what was passing in the world around them, to the realm of re-presentative intellect. An external phenomenon is thus translated into an internal conception." Hegel is describing the process of converting events into written words, which he holds as the highest form of thought. "Historiographers bind together the fleeting elements of story, and treasure them up for immortality in the Temple of Mnemosyne." It appears from Hegel's reasoning that the muse of memory does not accept any other idiom of thought than the written word, for she does not include "Legends, Ballad-stories, [and] Traditions" into her temple.[8]

For Hegel, not surprisingly, only those nations that have developed states possess the necessary conditions whereby "the prose of History" could be composed. Indeed, Hegel argues that the very act of writing about the past coincides with the appearance of historical events, meaning the activities of states. This is a restatement of the now classic rondo that says that "history begins with civilization because civilizations produced writing." Hegel observes, "In our language [German] the term History unites the objective with the subjective side," meaning that the word for "history" (*Geschichte*) comes from the word "to happen" (*geschehen*).[9] History "comprehends not less what has happened, than the narration of what has happened." In other words, there are no historical events unless they are narrated through written language. Like a tree falling in a forest, there is no history without narration.

Hegel argues that the narration produced by historians, while based on objective events, is an abstraction. Historians "change the events, the deeds, and the states of society with which they are conversant, into an object for the conceptive faculty."[10] This is what Hegel means when he suggests that history refers to both objective events and to subjective narration at the same time. Only written words, it seems, offer the type of objectification needed to produce a legitimate subjective narration of events. While this reasoning might make a certain amount of intuitive sense, it still does not explain *why* history is written, only *that* we have chosen to write, unless one is willing to accept that the Muses still determine what is the proper form of memory.

Ivan Illich and Barry Sanders need no references to Greek mythology to understand why historians write. "History becomes possible only when the Word turns into words," they write.

> Only verbatim traditions enable the historian to reconstruct the past. Only where words that were lost can be found again does the historiographer replace the storyteller. The historian's home is on the island of writing. He furnishes its inhabitants with subject matter about the past. The past that can be seized is related to writing. Beyond the island's shores, memories do not become words. Where no words are left behind, the historian finds no foundations for his reconstructions. In the absence of words, artifacts are silent. We have often felt frustrated, but we accept that prehistory cannot be read. No bridge can be constructed to span this chasm.[11]

Illich and Sanders imply that words are central to history as both primary and secondary sources. Historians re-create the past only when there are written records; they compose their secondary works only in written form. While some historians are willing to concede—unlike Illich and Sanders—that nonlinguistic sources can serve as primary sources, very few historians would accept a nonlinguistic secondary source as a legitimate substitute for a written account.

Illich and Sanders express a sentiment similar to Hegel's: that only words can capture the most meaningful events of the past. Although these ideas are forcefully presented, they still do not satisfactorily answer the question of why history *must* be written. If anything, these are expressions of faith, faith that only written words best capture reality. While these observations may seem ridiculously obvious to an historian, a mathematician might argue otherwise, that abstract symbols best capture reality. For a mathematician, words are too imprecise to accurately describe the world. Therefore, we cannot accept that words are superior to other idioms just by axiom or faith alone; we need to dig deeper, to look at the specific properties of words and writing, to understand the advantages and limitations of the idiom in which we are placing our faith.

Hegel, Illich, Sanders, and the entire discipline of history argue from axiom: historians write history because the Greeks wrote historia. In other words, history is written because historians say it is written. We prefer words either out of habit or out of faith that words are the highest level of thought. Our preference for words does not mean we adhere to some natural law—that history shall be written—but rather a form of circular logic, buttressed by convention.

Will historians use the computer to break this circle of convention? Will future historians reject the arguments and the faith in words expressed above? Or is Hegel correct, that history is linguistically and structurally inseparable from the written word? Before historians choose to communicate through computer visualizations, they will need to cleave writing from history.

Information Design

To repeat, historians choose to write because of tradition, convention, and faith. This choice is perfectly reasonable and legitimate; however, we should also recognize that there is nothing natural or axiomatic about writing about the past: it is only a preference. As such, our profession has made a collective "information design" decision. If "design" refers to the imposition of meaningful order,[12] then information design is the act of imposing meaningful order on ideas. "Information" is neither a substance nor a quantity, much as Claude Shannon and information theorists would like us to believe. Information is the product of the interaction between ideas, idioms of expression, and technology.[13]

I believe the process works something like this. Humans produce ideas from pure thought. The linguist and cognitive scientist Steven Pinker refers to this realm of pure thought as "mentalese." Rejecting the tradition in linguistics that contends that thought cannot exist apart from language—that language in fact creates thought—Pinker maintains that humans have a type of ur-thought that exists prior to language. He offers an example as a type of proof: "We have all had the experience of uttering or writing a sentence, then stopping and realizing that it wasn't exactly what we meant to say. To have that feeling, there has to be a 'what we meant to say' that is different from what we said." Language—though I would include any idiom—does not equate to thought, according to Pinker, who asks, "Are our thoughts [instead] couched in some silent medium of the brain . . . and merely clothed in words whenever we need to communicate them to a listener?"[14]

Communicating these thoughts may take several forms, which explains the wide variety of mediums. Presumably, mentalese or pure thought could be "clothed" in many forms: I could speak these thoughts, or write, or draw, or hum, or dance. Depending on my choice, the ur-thought is shaped by the resulting medium. Therefore, ideas expressed in writing will not be the same as those ideas expressed as a painting. Mentalese is formed into thought depending on the limitations and advantages of the medium.

How does one decide which medium to choose? How do I know that words are better than images or sounds? Some education researchers claim that there is no real difference between mediums of communication. These researchers champion the ideas of Howard Gardner, who argues in his book *Frames of Mind* that there does not exist a monolithic quantity called "intelligence" that can be measured and expressed by one number, as in an IQ test. Instead, Gardner argues that every human mind is a collection of "multiple intelligences," of spatial and linguistic and musical abilities among other cognitive skills. No two people share the exact combination of intelligences; thus no one number can compare the cognitive skills of two people of differing musical or spatial or kinesic ability.[15]

Gardner's work has deeply influenced both psychology and education and, as is typical with important ideas, has taken on a life of its own. Gardner has recently identified many of the myths surrounding his research.[16] I am especially troubled by one myth Gardner has not identified: the myth that multiple intelligences mean multiple conduits for information acquisition. Some education researchers who have absorbed Gardner's ideas claim that because the mind is made of multiple intelligences, every person acquires "information" differently, according to his or her unique cognitive apparatus. Therefore, so this argument goes, some people learn better if information is presented visually or aurally or if they have more tactile experiences than, say, through the written word alone. The task of the alert and empathetic teacher, then, is to determine the learner's appropriate channel for acquiring "the information."

The chief flaw of this argument, however, is the assumption that "the information" is the same regardless of which channel it passes through. According to this view, a cognitive medium is merely a passive conduit through which ideas pass unaltered by that conduit. This is similar to believing that a

German novel translated into English is the same text. However, any time a translator converts a text from one language to another, some nuances and meanings of the original are necessarily lost. Thus, the translated text—while similar and perfectly readable—is nevertheless different from the original.

The same holds true for ideas that have been "translated" into a different medium. Reading a score of Mozart's music is not the same as listening to the symphony. A script cannot convey the pitch, timbre, and pauses of an actor's performance. A verbal description of coffee cannot compare to the actual aroma of the bean. Because of these translation effects, it would be a mistake to conclude that written or aural or olfactory skill is a matter of individual preference and that the same "information" about music or theater or beverages can be acquired whatever the medium.

In any act of translation, some part of the "essence" of the idea is lost when transferred to the new medium.[17] A skillful translator seeks to retain as much of the essence of the original as the new medium will allow. The greater the retention of the essence, the greater the "isomorphism" between the two idioms. It is a mistake to conclude, however, that ideas expressed through different mediums reflect the identical information. This implies that all idioms are completely isomorphic, which as I demonstrate below is not true. The musician Elvis Costello is supposed to have described the difficulty of achieving complete isomorphism between mediums when he said, "Writing about music is like dancing about architecture." Mediums are different from each other precisely because of their lack of complete isomorphism.

Rather than thinking of visual or oral or musical ability as isomorphic conduits, it might be more useful to think of these skills as true mediums. Vibrations of sound, for example, are different when they pass through air or water or wood. There is no such thing as "sound" that remains unchanged whatever medium it passes through. The same holds true for communication idioms. Each medium has its own properties that shape the way the content is expressed, consequently changing the information. Each cognitive idiom possesses structural properties that make it distinct from others. Because of these differing properties, ideas expressed through them cannot remain unchanged; thus, the content in each case also cannot be the same.

If one adheres to the argument that "information" is the same regardless of the medium through which it is expressed, then it makes little difference how ideas are organized and presented, as long as the audience acquires the information. In order to appeal to different learning styles, a textbook designer or a teacher need only sprinkle any display with a variety of cognitive media. My contention, however, is that the medium *does* matter.

As I indicated before, Gardner's ideas are deeply evocative when one considers that the ideas emanating from the mind are expressed through a variety of idioms. These various forms of expression, however, are not equal to one another. It would be a mistake to assume that "information" is unchanged when translated into different media. Rather, one must learn to determine what is the best medium for didactically conveying certain types of thought. Sometimes words are best; sometimes pictures best accomplish the task; occasionally it is sound or movement. The choice depends on the types of ideas one wants to convey. Consider this example: you want to communicate geographical information to a surveyor about the topography of a region. You could write a verbal description, of course, but it makes more sense to compose a visual map of the area. This decision, to write or to draw, is what I mean by an information design decision.

The choice of technology makes this decision material. There can be no written words without parchment or ink or movable type. These material factors have some effect on the type of information created: writing on clay tables is a different type of activity than writing on papyrus.[18] Each technology has its limitations and advantages, but these are distinct from the medium. Thus, technology is an important part of the information design process, but is not the most important part of this process.

Words and Syntax

What are the properties of the written idiom of communication that historians find so appealing? To answer this question, we must break down the structure of prose into its component elements of words and syntax.[19]

Words

Words are multidimensional, complex, and nonlinear forms of information. Postmodern critics often decry the linearity of writing, a subject to which I will return shortly. While the syntax of writing may be linear, the semantics of the word—isolated from its linear chain—is dynamic and nonlinear. We are all familiar with the Chinese proverb "A picture is worth a thousand words." Critics of the word—including a fair number of my students—often evoke this saying to "prove" that written words are inefficient ways to communicate. However, the complexity and efficiency of words lies beneath their surface. "The word," according to Rosenstone, "can provide vast amounts of data in a small space. The word can generalize, talk of great abstractions like revolution, evolution, and progress, and make us believe that these things exist."[20] He notes that attempting to convey such concepts through film images, for example, proves very difficult, for images are not as efficient at communicating generalizations. Think of the way historians generalize about complex phenomena in only a few short words: "renaissance," "crisis," "industrial revolution," "patriarchy." Thus, it seems that, in some cases, a word might be worth a thousand pictures.

The mathematician and cognitive scientist Douglas Hofstadter argues that words accomplish this task since they are surrounded by a "halo" of meaning. He notes that mathematicians tend to distrust words since they are so full of meaning and are therefore "imprecise." Hofstadter observes that Euclid preferred the abstract symbols of mathematics "for an inevitable consequence of his using ordinary words was that some of the images conjured up by those words crept into the proofs which he created."[21] Unlike words, mathematical symbols are more "precise" and "efficient" since they are stripped of excess connotations and meanings.

Hofstadter himself delights in words, in their layers of meaning and connotation. He devotes one of his recent books, *Le Ton beau de Marot,* to the phenomenon of translation and the halos around words. "A word," he writes, "being the name of a concept, and a concept being a class of items linked by analogy, and people by nature being creative and ever finding new analogies, a word's connotations are consequently oozing continually outwards to form an ever-larger and blurrier nebula as more and more analogies are recognized. . . . Words have halos."[22] Those of us who use the *Oxford English Dictionary* understand that words have depth and history, an archeology of meaning that changes at each stratum as one descends into their etymology. In my classes, I often take a word, such as "civilization" or "revolution" or "global," and write the definitions, meanings, and connotations of the word all around it, with criss-crossing lines connecting the connotations, in a very complex, nonlinear manner. The point of this exercise is to demonstrate that the semantics of a word swirls around it like a sphere or cloud. Meaning does not always line up under a word as in a dictionary.

This inherent complexity of the word is not readily apparent by surface appearance alone, for much of the information conveyed through words is unseen. This is because words are "high-context," and much of their meaning is "understood." The anthropologist Edward T. Hall defined "high-context" as a form of communication "in which most of the information is either in the physical context or internalized in the person, while very little is in the coded, explicit, transmitted part of the message." In contrast, "a low context communication is just the opposite; i.e. the mass of the information is vested in the explicit code."[23] Thus, an example of high-context communication is a glance shared by a husband and wife. In the explicit action of the glance, very little information is apparent to one who does not understand the shared context between the couple. The couple, however, understands the unstated meaning surrounding the glance by "filling in" the meaning. An example of low-context communication is an Internet URL: confuse one period for a comma, one capital letter for a lowercase letter, and the computer will not "understand." One cannot say to a computer, "You know what I meant!" because all of the meaning is encoded in the letters of the URL.

Historians rely on high-context communication anytime they compose a history. When I write "Golden Age," entire vistas of information are opened up in the mind of the reader. Consider also how choice of words influences how historians construct the past. Was Columbus's voyage an "heroic achievement" or a "genocidal tragedy"? The difference between these words are the meanings they evoke. For such evocation to occur, however, the reader must activate them; this is why words are high-context.

While there are certainly many examples of low-context words—technical jargon, for example—in general, words require that the reader "understand" much of the communication that is not explicitly presented in the visible code. To make this property of written words clearer, compare words to mathematical symbols. In the 1970s, historians interested in quantitative methods argued that numbers and mathematical symbols were a "better" idiom with which to express ideas about the past. "The advantage of quantitative history," argued Roderick Floud, "in contrast to qualitative impressionistic history, is that its systems and methods of classification, the assumptions it uses and the patterns it imposes, are stated and clear; one does not have to see into the mind of the historian, or follow his thought processes, to understand quantitative history."[24] Words are "impressionistic," it seems, since they require more high-context understanding between the minds of historians.

Mathematical symbols, in contrast, are low-context. Devotees of mathematics believe that numerical symbols are "universal," which is another way of saying "decontextualized." Think of the symbol "7." That symbol can be deciphered by speakers of many different languages, even if they have different names for the symbol. Numerals, algebraic symbols, and mathematical syntax are all low-context, since the bulk of the meaning of the communication is stated in the explicit code; there is a much smaller halo of meaning needed for understanding. When mathematicians describe their idiom as elegant, precise communication,[25] they are referring to the relatively low-context communication of their symbols. Mathematicians favor precision, parsimony, Occam's razor. This is one way of saying that their method of communication lacks the swirling halo of meaning around its symbols. This is what Hofstadter means when he says mathematicians distrust the extraneous images and meanings that are central to words, in favor of stripped-down, context-free symbols. If mathematics is elegant and precise, does this mean that words are "clumsy" and "imprecise"? The answer is "yes" if one values low-context communication and "no" if one values high-context communication.[26]

Mathematicians and writers do share at least one commonality: their mediums are both abstractions. Written words, in fact, are abstractions twice removed from reality. A written word refers to a spoken sound, which in turn refers to something in the external world. When an historian writes the word "war," that symbol is an abstraction that refers to a spoken sound, which is itself an abstraction for an entire range of violent human actions.[27] Thus, using written words to reconstruct the past is an exercise in abstraction; our words become objects that we mentally manipulate as if they were tangible and real. When students complain that history books are dry and boring, but historical films somehow "make the past come to life," they might be expressing a dislike for the abstractions of written words—not realizing, of course, that a film is also an abstraction of the past.

Syntax

While words are nonlinear and complex, their syntactical arrangement is linear and one-dimensional. Writing is the process of taking nonlinear, complex, abstract objects (words) and placing them in linear order. One of the great difficulties for any writer is learning how to "line up" those nonlinear objects. In fact, one could define "writer's block" as the inability to line up words properly. A gifted student in my history of economic thought class came to me before the first essay was due with a problem. She had so many ideas and connections she wished to explore that she could not satisfactorily organize her ideas. She asked instead if she could create a "word collage," a pastiche of words that attempted to display the complexity of her thinking. This student had composed a hypertext essay for me in another class; I would not have allowed any other student to propose such a radical idea, but since I knew she was a gifted and creative writer capable of well-composed traditional compositions, I was willing to let her try a nonlinear form of writing. The final product was good (I gave her a B) but more importantly, the exercise taught us both an important lesson about writing: that to engage in the practice of writing means taking essentially simultaneous thoughts and ideas about complex nonlinear objects and determining a linear order for them.

For at the root of language is syntax, and syntax is sequence. The act of placing a noun and verb together is a process of linearizing. Every language, of course, has its own particular syntax; the German language occasionally places verbs at the end of sentences, whereas in English verbs usually trail closely behind nouns. Nor am I discussing Noam Chomsky's notion of syntax, the unconscious rules that generate grammar. Instead, I am referring to the tendency of written languages to arrange words in sequential order. Chinese arranges words up and down, English left to right, Arabic right to left. In each case, the complex, halo-enshrouded words line up in sequential order. The word "I" has an extremely complex halo of meaning surrounding it, as does the equally complex word "am." When I put these words together, "I am" linearizing nonlinear concepts.

Writing cannot help but be linear, for two reasons. First, the stream of speech—to which writing refers—is essentially linear; that is, we speak in sequence. While the stories we tell through words and language may meander and make reference to nonsequential or nonlinear events, the sequence of utterances is always linear. For example, I could write "I was born tomorrow, then my son was born before me." While the account is (nonsensically) nonlinear, the action of speaking or writing is linear: one utterance, one sound, one word follows after another. Writing makes this essential linearity visually apparent.

While language and writing may be linear, as Carlyle understood, the reality both refer to is not. "There is nothing lineal or sequential," writes Marshall McLuhan, "about the total field of awareness that exists in any moment of consciousness."[28] This is because the reality that surrounds us is not sequential. According to the psychologist Rudolf Arnheim, humans perceive the world as a "four-dimensional world of [both] sequence and spatial simultaneity." When describing this multidimensional reality with language and writing, we in effect cut "one-dimensional paths through the spatial landscape . . . [dismantling] the simultaneity" of reality.[29] This argument is similar to that of Carlyle, who notes that writers of history "thread the world with single lines of a few els in length." While "consciousness is not a verbal process," says McLuhan, those who speak and write treat it like it is. If one has a hammer, the world looks like a nail; if one thinks through language and writing, the whole world appears in sequence.

The second reason that writing is linear is that it is displayed on a flat surface. Different cultures have produced writing systems with their own conventions of reading order. In the West, we are accustomed to reading from left to right, in descending order. In Arabic and Hebrew, however, the reading order is from right to left. In Chinese, the order is from top to bottom. In each of these cases, the syntax is one-dimensional (one word next to another) and not two-dimensional (words placed next to and on top of each other as on a Cartesian grid). Nor has there been a writing system where the syntax was in three dimensions: words placed up, down, and out.

Whether because of convention or essential principle, writing is displayed on flat surfaces. Whether that surface is clay, papyrus, silk, parchment, and yes, even the computer screen, syntax remains a one-dimensional property. When we write or read, we connect words and sentences linearly. While words have certainly been featured on three-dimensional objects—such as words on sculpture—the connection between words always unfolds on the flat surfaces of those objects. We could, theoretically, arrange words in three-dimensional space, but before this could truly constitute a three-dimensional syntax, written words themselves would need to be three-dimensional. That is, three-dimensional words would not be merely decorations of two-dimensional words; the extra dimension would be intrinsic to meaning. The position of the word, its location rotated on an axis, would be as important as its position in a (linear) sentence. Of course, such a three-dimensional written syntax is only a fantasy, for no such system exists except as theory. In my estimation, a three-dimensional syntax could not even be labeled "writing."

Whatever the language, whatever the writing surface, whatever the reading order, syntax is one-dimensional. The art historian John Kissick contends that the inventors of the first writing systems understood that linguistic sequence was easier to display on two-dimensional surfaces rather than on a three-dimensional medium such as sculpture. "Because a full understanding of an object depends on its being observed from various angles, the ancient Egyptians probably decided that three-dimensional images were poor conductors of progressive storyline";[30] thus their highly visual writing system was composed on flat surfaces. If speech is sequential and if writing follows from speech, then the medium upon which it is composed must be conducive to this property.

Literate cultures typically assume sequence to be the highest form of thought. "During all our centuries of phonetic literacy," notes McLuhan, "we have favored the chain of inference as the mark of logic and reason." Perhaps this is why historians value writing: for the logic and reasoning it enables. "Our ideas of cause-and-effect in the literate West," says McLuhan, "have long been in the form of things in sequence and succession."[31] Stated another way, since historians write, syntax shapes the sequence of cause and effect relationships between past events that we create.

If history were simply a matter of listing events in chronological order, then the question of sequence would be moot. However, historians do more than list events; we try to understand the meaning, significance, and relationships between those events. "History" is analytic; it is not mere chronicle.

Most historians understand that events unfold in much more complex ways than simple chains of causation. Few would contend that events always unfold as they do in a linear sentence, for we do not wish to fall into the trap of *post hoc, ergo propter hoc*. Nevertheless, there is a tradition in the philosophy of history that holds that cause and effect relationships are linear and "chainlike." Further, because we write, it is difficult to convey events that occur simultaneously. While we can write "The war, economic depression, and financial collapse occurred at the same time," we can list the events only one at a time, never "at the same time." This is, in part, Carlyle's frustration: the idiom of writing makes it very difficult to translate simultaneity into sequence.

Historians construct their narrative accounts in the form of prose, that is, words arranged in linear sentences organized into sequential paragraphs. Consider the events leading up to the Great War in 1914. A typical narrative might line up this way:

> The Great War began after structural weaknesses in the European alliance system, spurred on by long-standing colonial and economic competition, caused the collapse of the Bismarckian system. At the same time, virulent nationalism exacerbated the situation. These factors combined to create two rival blocs, while an arms race between Britain and Germany, as well as several diplomatic crises, such as the Moroccan Crisis and the Balkan Wars, fueled distrust between the European powers. Then, after Serbian gunman Gavrilo Princip shot Austrian archduke Francis Ferdinand, Austria sought to punish Serbia for the deed. Germany backed Austria, which triggered Russian concerns, which set in motion a complex cascade of diplomatic action, culminating in several states instituting mobilization plans.

With each word, with each sentence, I have taken a number of complex, abstract, and mutually inclusive concepts and lined them up. While I could add more words and sentences to clarify and expand my narrative, this would have the effect of "cutting more lines" across the four-dimensional structure of early twentieth-century Europe.

Even if we do not believe that events unfold in chainlike procession and that the events we list have no direct causal connection, the medium of writing nevertheless imposes such chainlike limits on our abstractions. Since "to write" means "to line up," we must make choices about which words will go in which sequence, for those choices have consequences for the final shape of that "history." Consider some examples of the basic syntax of my account: "war began," "gunman shot," and "Germany backed." Taken separately, each word is a complex of connotations and meanings that I must place in one-dimensional order. The shortest distance between subjects and verbs—the stuff of language—is a line.

Further, I used words such as "caused" and "allowed," which imply linear causation, but I also used words such as "as well as" and "while," which imply events occurring simultaneously, without any necessary causal connection. Because of the limitations of the idiom, even if I were describing simultaneous events, I still must select a linear order in which to place them. Because I write, I have to create the fiction of a linear order.

Does this order matter in historical thought? Could I, for example, change the order of events? Would it make more sense to argue that imperial competition was spurred on by the collapse of the Bismarckian system? Could I write about Sarajevo first, then the Balkan Wars, then the Moroccan Crisis, in effect working backwards? Could I list the short-term causes first, then list the long-term factors? What would I be implying about the causes of the war by doing so? Would I reach the same conclusions about causation were I to alter the order? Because the historian must "line everything up" in a written account, the order is an important choice, as significant as the choice of words. Even if we deny that the linear procession of words implies linear causal connections, with each sentence we write we engage in what Arnheim describes as cutting one-dimensional paths across the four-dimensional complexity of the past.[32]

Prose into Image

I once attended a conference at which the invited speaker bragged that he had eliminated linearity from his courses. The audience nodded approvingly, as if to agree that linear thinking was a virus that had to be purged from the academic body. I raised my hand during the question-and-answer session and asked the apparently unpopular question "What is wrong with linear thinking?" I did not read Carlyle believing that he wished to eradicate linear thinking; he was, rather, expressing an awareness of the limitations of prose as a medium of thought in history. As I argue in the next chapter, all mediums of thought have limitations: there is no Platonic medium that exactly and perfectly represents thought. Thus, I do not wish to advocate the elimination of either writing or linear thinking, only that we understand their limitations without illusion, if only to all the more appreciate their strengths. Moreover, it seems to me that there are many instances when we want to simplify simultaneity into sequence. That is, there are many instances when writing and linear thinking are beneficial and necessary. An historical narrative may very well be one of those instances.

In some circles, this is an unpopular notion. There is a recent tradition in Western thought that distrusts both writing and linear thinking. McLuhan faults writing for much that is wrong with the West. "Only alphabetic cultures," he writes, "have ever mastered connected lineal sequences as pervasive forms of psychic and social organization. The breaking up of every kind of experience into uniform units in order to produce faster action and change of form (applied knowledge) has been the secret of Western power over man and nature alike." Linear thinking, it seems, is a type of cognitive imperialism. "That is the reason why our Western industrial programs have quite involuntarily been so militant, and our military programs have been so industrial. Both are shaped by the alphabet in their technique of transformation and control by making all situations uniform and continuous."[33] Leonard Shlain contends that alphabets are masculine, since they emphasize the linear and sequential portions of the brain's hemispheres. On medical and biological grounds, Shlain argues that the invention of the alphabet thereby facilitated the creation of patriarchy, by overwhelming the right-brain, feminine, imagistic hemisphere.[34] The art educator Betty Edwards believes that the left brain consciously censors the right brain, thus dampening the potential for human creativity.[35] Although these authors penned thousands of words to explain their perspectives, they maintain that written linear thinking is masculine, Western, imperialistic, and wrong.

Theorists working with hypertext claim to have solved many of these limitations of linear, sequential prose. Hypertext refers to the theoretical ability to digitally connect words in a web, not a linear chain. Hypertext is, of course, a common feature of most Web sites. Navigating around the Internet involves clicking on a highlighted word that often sends one to a completely different page of the site or, if the site is linked, to another site entirely. In theory, then, a hypertext has no beginning, middle, or end. A reader can enter into the text anywhere, read in any direction, and exit at any point. The implication is that hypertext has eliminated the linear progression implied by the successive pages and chapters of a printed book, calling into question the "fiction of the line" that is printed writing.

Proponents of hypertext promise that the technique of writing on the computer screen will allow us to finally break up the linearity of writing.[36] By providing highlighted words and phrases as links to other Web pages, hypertext gives the reader unprecedented power over the direction of the story, a power traditionally held by the writer, who, by his linear choices, guides the reader along the narrative path. Rather than concerning themselves with "lining up" ideas in sequential order, so this argument goes, writers of hypertext need not worry about the order of events. The writer instead allows the reader to choose the reading path she desires, absolving the writer of having to decide the path or to choose the causal connections.

Champions of hypertext find antecedents in the novels of Laurence Sterne, James Joyce, and Milorad Pavic, and theoretical support from Jacques Derrida, Michel Foucault, and Roland Barthes. Sterne's book, *Tristram Shandy,* features a meandering, twisting, some might say aimless, plot. The author moves forward and backward in time, in fact drawing a diagram that displays this meandering plot. *Tristram Shandy* is not completely hypertextual, however, since readers are not invited to choose their own reading paths. Theorists contend that Sterne and later modernist writers such as Joyce and T.S. Eliot sought to "undermine the inherent consecutiveness of language, frustrating the reader's normal expectation of a sequence."[37] These writers intuited the hypertextual writing space, but were inhibited by the technology of print.

Milorad Pavic's books, most notably *The Dictionary of the Khazars,* appear more hypertextual, since the reader must make actual choices about the reading order. In that novel, the reader must create the plot of the story by reading entries from three dictionaries. In the introduction, Pavic says that readers can read each entry as printed, follow common entries in each dictionary, or read any or all parts of the book in whatever order they choose. The reader may treat the text like a lexicon, looking up words when the need arises, or like a novel, with each section serving as chapters to be read in traditional fashion. In Pavic's novels, the reader's choice of reading path is as important to the plot of the story as the writer's intentions.

Hypertext presents important implications for a discipline such as history that depends on writing. Imagine the implications of this writing technique for the composition of an historical account. In theory, a history written in this hypertextual fashion would permit the reader to choose the path of events. This explains my emphasis above on the significance of sequential order in historical writing. While an historian might assemble blocks of texts, the reader would choose the connections between those blocks. Thus, the final narrative would be as much the reader's decision as the historian's. How comfortable will we be handing over narrative choice—and, thus, analytic control—to our readers? If historians wish to compose histories in a hypertext environment, what will happen to our traditional notions of time and causation, bound as they are to linear modes of thought?

While hypertext composition has clearly altered the experience of reading text, it might be a stretch to conclude that the medium has "overcome" the linearity of print. This is because hypertext has yet to alter either words or syntax, the foundations of language. Hypertextual writing most certainly alters our experience of prose by altering our Western sense of transition between paragraphs, since the nonlinear reading choices appear to flow between paragraphs. Barthes argues that nonlinear reading and writing is based on jumbling up "lexia," blocks of text, which for Barthes and hypertext theorists are the building blocks of hypertextual writing. The computer, however, has done little to significantly change the nature of either words or syntax. When a reader clicks on a word on the screen that links him to some other place, he is not really engaging in a new form of syntax. Those lexia, those blocks of text, are still made up of words organized into sentences. Instead, by clicking on a word, the reader sees before him connections and connotations that that word suggests. Instead of a new syntax, he views a low-context technique of displaying the halo of meaning surrounding the word. The fundamental pattern of word and syntax, however, remains basically the same, and that pattern is one-dimensional and linear.

Nevertheless, champions of hypertext seem positively giddy about the idea that the line—meaning linear arguments, linear plots, and linear texts—cannot withstand the nonlinearity of the computer. Derrida proclaims "the end to the line" when he writes that "the end of linear writing is indeed the end of the book." Rather than being morose, George Landow notes, "writers on hypertext are downright celebratory" about the death of the line. Critical theorists, according to this argument, lived during the last dying days of the line and therefore wrote about "the limitation—indeed, the exhaustion—of the culture of print. They write from an awareness of limitation and short-coming, and from moody nostalgia . . . at the losses their disillusionment has brought and will bring."[38] In fact, it seems these same mourners long to hasten the final death, if only to put the line out of its misery.

Hypertext theorists, although responding to the same perceived death knell, "glory in possibility, excited by the future of textuality, knowledge, and writing." The computer promises these theorists an afterlife for the text, a reincarnation on a nonlinear writing surface. "Most poststructuralists write from within the twilight of a wished-for coming day," concludes Landow; "most writers of hypertext write of many of the same things from within the dawn."[39]

I am not convinced that the line is dead and writing obsolete. Outside a narrow range of nonlinear texts, there are countless linear textual moments. Consider directions; if I want to get to your house, if I want to bake a cake, if I want to properly assemble one of my son's toys, then I want a linear text. Before I drive to your home, I want you—the "author"—to compose a step-by-step procession controlled by you; if I am baking, I want to see the beginning, middle, and end of the recipe; if I were to follow my own "reading path" and not the one suggested by the toy manufacturer, then there is a very good chance my son will never be able to play with the toy. To write on the computer screen does not necessarily mean abandoning the line.

In seeking to remove the "limitations" of the printed word, those who wish to connect words in a hypertextual fashion seem to want writing to act more spatial and "imagelike." Rudolf Arnheim (not a deconstructionist) distinguishes linear thought from visual thinking. He argues, sensibly, that when employing linear thought, the mind connects elements as in a chain. When employing visual thought, the mind connects these elements as in a web. However, Arnheim then concludes that the latter type of thinking is "better" than the former. "The principle virtue of the visual medium," Arnheim writes, "is that of representing shapes [of thought] in two-dimensional and three-dimensional space, as compared with the one-dimensional sequence of . . . language."[40] I believe advocates for hypertext writing wish to transform one-dimensional linear writing into a two- or even three-dimensional medium, one that connects words not as a chain but as a web. It would seem, then, that hypertext advocates wish to stuff the "square peg" of writing into the "round hole" of visualization.

At the very least, the formal structure of a hypertext composition is multidimensional. Jay David Bolter notes that one can take a hypertext composition —he favors "Afternoon" by Michael Joyce—and represent the structure of the story as a diagram reflecting the hundreds of blocks of text and the hundreds of possible links from which a reader might connect those blocks. "The reader," observes Bolter, "never sees this diagrammed structure," the structure remaining hidden like the plumbing underneath a city. Instead, "the reader's experience of 'Afternoon' is one-dimensional, as he or she follows paths from one episode to another." Again, because it is a written medium, hypertext retains its one-dimensionality and linearity. To imagine the multidimensional connections between episodes, "the reader must gain an intuition of the spatial structure as he or she proceeds in time."[41]

One could easily make visible such a structure as an interface for the reader. In fact, that hidden diagrammatic structure looks very similar to a concept map, a type of visualization explored in chapter 5. The reader might then select specific episodes from the structure and thus see the multidimensional whole while linearly reading one of its parts. One could even diagram a hypertextual narrative in three dimensions, with each level reflecting a different perspective on the whole. For example, Bolter envisions a three-dimensional structure of the story of Oedipus, in which one level of the story is from the perspective of a shepherd, one from Oedipus, and one from an Olympian god.[42] A reader might then click onto those episodes in any order and at any levels he wished. Blocks of text—while read in one dimension—connect to each other in multiple dimensions.

If hypertext is a hybrid type of composition that hovers between one- and two-dimensions, can we really continue to call this writing? This would be like changing the rules of basketball by saying the game will now be played by eleven players on a grassy field with an oval ball where tackling is permitted. Is this still basketball or a completely different game? If the goal of hypertext is to refashion writing so as to be multidimensional and spatial—to more easily depict simultaneity—then one must first refashion the syntax of writing. That is, one would need to begin to read, write, and connect words in more than one dimension. Were this to occur, I contend, we would no longer be looking at writing but at some other type of representation of thought, something more like an abstract visualization.

Rather than attempting to change "prose into image" through the postmodern alchemy of hypertext, it might be easier to simply employ an idiom whose syntax is already two- or three-dimensional. If multidimensional spatial thinking better captures a concept or situation, then one might be better off thinking visually rather than attempting to convert a linear idiom into something it is not. At the very least, the fact that some writers and theorists wish to remake linear prose into a visual, spatial, multidimensional medium signals the receptivity of our culture to visualization and visual thinking.

As I argued above, there are many instances when a linear, sequential presentation is necessary and desirable. However, there are also moments when a visual display organizes thought and information better than linear written prose. Historians must carefully consider their choices, for our idiom of thought and communication is a matter of conscious choice. Whatever the choice, it is surely a stretch to conclude that one idiom of thought is superior to the other, since linear and spatial thinking are both part of every human's multiple intelligences. A modern day Carlyle might choose to represent the Chaos of Being in a medium other than writing, but this need not mean that writing has no place in his cognitive toolbox.

Chapter Two

Visualization As an Alternative to Prose

Written prose is linear, one-dimensional, confined to sequential chains, and—if Carlyle, McLuhan, and Arnheim are to be believed—ill-equipped to represent the multidimensional complexity of thought and experience. Historians rarely recognize these limitations and constraints of their medium of choice, and when they do, like Carlyle, they choose to write anyway. This choice has consequences. Written prose is not only a means of communication; because of its structural properties, writing shapes our thoughts, organizing our ideas like a template or a filter. When the past is pressed through the template of prose, "history" is created.

Despite the criticisms from McLuhan and others, there is nothing intrinsically wrong with either unidimensionality or sequence. I have made a conscious choice to employ prose as my medium of thought and as my organizational template for this book, in part because it is expected of me as an historian. But I also find prose to be an elegant, supple form of communication, one that I enjoy working with very much. The one-dimensional linear properties of prose are constraining to be sure, but this is not the point: every medium constrains our thinking. Like an artist who is constrained by her choice of marble, acrylic, or charcoal, the historian is constrained by the medium in which she chooses to work. Because we think and communicate with symbols and signs, we can never hope to perfectly represent the Platonic realm of "pure thought." We are forced to choose which forms of communication—which constraints and limitations on our thinking—are more acceptable than others.

What if Ph.D. advisers, professional organizations, and journal editors allowed historians to behave like artists and choose their medium of thought? What if historians were permitted to choose the communicative constraints under which they work? If allowed to make such an informed choice, how long will historians continue to accept the limitations of prose, especially since "highly technological societies are experiencing a phase of Copernican change from the dominance of language to the hegemony of images"?[1] Such a shift in our discipline would be momentous, for if historians filtered the past through some other medium of thought—such as visualization—we would alter our understanding of that past, and perhaps the definition of "history" itself.

The choice might already have been made for us, since more and more "information" in the Information Age is visual and spatial. It hardly needs to be stated that ours is a society awash in images, from motion pictures and print advertisements, billboards and television shows, to the now ubiquitous Diamondvision screens that lord over sports stadiums. It seems that in this century, Western culture has witnessed a shift in the ratio between written, spoken, and visual information. If we could inventory the distribution and configuration of these forms of information in a society, we would probably discover that "highly technological societies" have more visual information than, say, Victorian Britain or Periclean Athens.

After the pronouncements of McLuhan, such observations do not appear original, yet their implications seem not to have affected the discipline of history. Historians, despite the visual culture that swirls around us, have hardly been touched by that culture. When historians do employ television, films, and other older visual technologies, they are used to supplement our textual culture; while there are certainly exceptions, historians generally do not allow their thoughts to be organized and constrained by visual images.

The computer might well be the next technology in a long line of technologies that historians press into the service of our textual culture. Most historians choose to view the computer as a word processor, a mail system, an electronic book, or a digital archive for storing primary sources. This decision is not shared by all residents of cyberspace, however, since some computer scientists and Web designers maintain that in the realm of computing there is "a shift of information processing from the lexical to the spatial realm."[2] This means that for information designers, businesspeople, researchers, and other residents of cyberspace, written prose is too slow and cumbersome to handle the enormous flow of data and information that moves through the electronic ether. Computer professionals—and the society at large—appear to be turning away from writing and prose because they believe it to be an inefficient transmitter of information.

In contrast, visual displays of data increasingly appear to be the preferred template for organizing information. A visualization is a two- or three-dimensional image that organizes and communicates meaningful information. Visualization allows the information designer to represent simultaneity, multidimensionality, pattern, and nonlinearity with a speed and efficiency that prose cannot capture. Let me state categorically that the title of this chapter does not mean that visualization is a superior form of communication, only that it is an alternative, that it offers different constraints on our thinking. Given the constraints of written prose, and if allowed an informed choice, will historians seek an alternative to prose in the form of visualization?

Attitudes Toward Visualization

As matters currently stand, the answer to that last question would appear to be no. As a rule, historians tend to distrust any type of visual information. The chief reason for this was explored in the previous chapter: historians have long defined the discipline in terms of written evidence and prose. It is true that historians on occasion use visual information such as maps, diagrams, and graphs as a way to illustrate written composition. These visual displays, however, typically serve as supplements to the written prose that organizes our thoughts about the past.

Moreover, historians often look upon these supplements as unwelcomed intrusions into the pure form of the prose. Alexander Stille expresses a commonly held belief among historians about visual illustrations. Reviewing an American history textbook for the middle-school level, Stille bemoans the increasing use of charts, diagrams, and other "graphics" that seem to overwhelm these texts. "Occasionally," he observes,

> such material can be helpful, but more often than not it is distracting, boring, and trivial, cutting down space for a more serious treatment of events. The hundreds of graphic presentations [in the fifth-grade text he was reviewing] seem designed not so much to interest children as to sell the book to teachers and education administrators who are more likely to flip through a prospective textbook looking for "special features" than to read it.[3]

While Stille grants that visual information might be occasionally helpful, he believes that words are by definition better able to convey "serious" information. For Stille, "graphics" are merely background noise that interrupt the more meaningful ideas expressed in words. His critique of "graphics" in textbooks is well taken, for as I will demonstrate below some visual information is better designed than others. As in a critique of written style and composition, one must be prepared to make similar stylistic comments about visual thought and composition. However, I suspect that Stille's discomfort with visual information is rooted in a belief that the visual cannot be as rigorous as the written. Inasmuch as the visual is a supplement to the written, it stands in a subordinate position.

Stille claims that the graphics in the textbook he is reviewing cannot be of interest to children. Yet textbook designers have precisely that goal in mind— capturing the interest of children— when they inundate texts with visual information. These designers are influenced by the mythologies of multiple intelligences (MI), which were outlined in the previous chapter. To summarize this position, some MI advocates believe that children learn through a variety of cognitive channels. Some students learn better through visual information than through text, so including graphics in a text is a way to appeal to those learners. I have already noted that, while some students will surely benefit from this well-intentioned pedagogical style, this approach sometimes fails to take into consideration the "translation effects" between different cognitive media: that information conveyed through writing is not necessarily the same as information conveyed in visual form. Further, some who claim to champion multiple intelligences often distort these ideas into a form of education that is mere "infotainment."

Frequently, advocates who include visual information in education do so in the belief that the visual is more "interesting" than written text. According to the adult education specialist William Draves, "we are living in an age of sensory stimulation, and being able to keep people's attention is helped by giving them different kinds of sensory stimulation."[4] His is not an isolated opinion. Education researchers, classroom teachers, and business trainers often argue that the use of visual information in a presentation "enlivens" what would otherwise be a dull lecture or boring text. Visual graphics "break up" monotonous blocks of text, making education and training more "interesting." Images seem especially well suited to grabbing the viewer's attention and holding on to it, in a way that written information cannot. One must use pictures, according to this view, to capture the attention of a learner who would otherwise be bored by words and writing.

On the surface, this second approach to visual information sounds more sympathetic than Stille's. However, I believe it to be just as dismissive. Beneath this enthusiastic support for visual displays of information is the sense that the written text—as boring as it might be—is still the real carrier of the meaningful information. In his book *Silicon Dreams,* Robert Lucky admits, "The pictures [in his book] relieve the visual monotony of endless font. Almost none of the pictures or diagrams in this book conveys substantive information. They are often placed simply to moderate the visual flow [of the words]." When making a speech or presentation, Lucky notes that his words contain the real information, while the pictures are merely "an attention device." Yet in the end, Lucky's audiences seem to remember the pictures more than the words, for "we have been well trained on the need for a constant flow of diversionary pictures."[5]

Images, it seems, are a condiment to the meatier, if unpalatable, words; visual information merely makes linguistic information easier to digest. To my way of thinking, this approach to images respects neither visual information nor written information. While images might appear more interesting, in these cases the visual remains in a subordinate position to the written. If advocates for visual information believe it to be merely attention-grabbing and entertaining, historians have every reason to treat visualization as an inferior form of thought and communication.

While visual graphics increasingly overwhelm educational materials, there are very few instances in the educational experience where the visual is treated on an equal pedagogical footing with the written. This might also explain why historians tend to distrust visual information: our educational experiences have given us little cause to value images over words. Even as diversionary and attention-grabbing images invade classrooms, educational curricula continue to emphasize linguistic and mathematical competency, as measured by such instruments as standardized tests. A child's education contains very few courses in "visual competency" outside of art classes and a smattering of elective courses, such as photography or "mass media." Art classes, however, do not share the same stature as courses in writing and mathematics. If "Johnny can't read," the entire society wrings its hands over the problems of schools and frets over Johnny's competitiveness. If "Johnny can't draw," no one bats an eye. Perhaps this explains why the art teacher in many schools is an overworked itinerant whose contact with children comes only once or twice a week. In times of budget crisis, art classes are among the easiest to cut.

Our educational institutions do not insist that students engage in a systematic study of the visual for one of two reasons. First, educators have traditionally equated the visual with antischooling. Visual images are often associated with television, video games, movies, and other flotsam of mass culture. Schoolchildren who seek out "the movie version" rather than reading the book are accused of cutting corners. "Looking at the pictures" is often associated with a preliterate phase of development, something little kids do with books before they learn to read the words. Even as more visual material enters classroom experience, children are rarely asked to think as seriously and formally about images as they do about words or numbers.

A second, and closely related, reason that educational institutions overlook the visual is that it is often identified as an "enrichment experience" and not as a core cognitive competency. Art appreciation courses perhaps make one a more "cultured" person, but curriculum designers assume such knowledge to be less practical, less useful, and thus not important enough to be included as part of basic education. If Gardner's multiple intelligences theory has done anything, it has demonstrated that visual thinking and spatialization skills are as important in childhood development as linguistic or mathematical skill.[6]

Moreover, these visual skills serve as more than mere cultural enrichment. The sociologist and art critic Kathryn Henderson notes that in many scientific disciplines, in mathematics, and in engineering, visual skill is an important core competency.

> My years spent learning to sketch and draw made it clear to me that artistic rendering skills were not enrichment frills that were so trivial that school boards could cut them with impunity. I suspected, rather, that they were connected to cognitive skills as basic as mathematics and verbal literacy and equally applicable to all sorts of problem solving—in math and science as well as the visual arts.[7]

Many first-year engineering students have flunked out of the program because they lack strong three-dimensional spatial visualization skills, an absolutely essential requirement for any engineer who wishes to draw or even read engineering design schematics. So acute is the problem that two professors at Michigan Tech offer classes in spatial visualization and have written a text on the subject.[8] One wonders whether math and science scores would improve if students were given more formal visual training at the elementary and secondary levels.

Graphing mathematical equations, drawing what one observes under a microscope, or diagramming an economic model are all tasks that require visual skill or at least the ability to visualize abstract information. This suggests that the boundary between "art" and "visualization" is an artificial one. Renaissance artists such as Leonardo Da Vinci and Albrecht Dürer were at home with both "artistic" images and more scientific "nonartistic" images, with little boundary separating the two domains. The art historian James Elkins attempts to break down this traditional boundary between art images and "nonart images"—such as diagrams, schematics, charts, and maps—by arguing that the systematic study of the former can be applied to the latter.[9] In his work, Elkins employs art historical techniques to examine images created in such seemingly "nonartistic" disciplines as crystallography. More importantly, he attempts to systematize the study of images, a crucial step in making visualization as legitimate as the study of words or numbers.

Sensing a lack of systematic study of the visual at my own institution, I designed a course titled Visual Thinking, which allowed students to study the visualization of information. My goal was to create a visual composition course similar to an English 101 composition course. My students and I carefully studied the structural properties of maps, diagrams, organizational charts, and various styles of graphs. We explored techniques for drawing visual information and learned that "drawing" need not mean "realistically rendering concrete objects," a rather narrow definition of visual thinking.

One of the more valuable exercises we engaged in focused on drawing up a list of stylistic "rules of thumb" for visual thinking, similar to the types of stylistic rules found in writing guides. Not surprisingly, our formal rules for visualization sounded very similar to the rules of writing:

- Avoid clutter: make any visualization simple, but complex enough to explain your ideas.
- A visual display of information must convey the idea in its entirety, else it is a mere illustration.
- Know your audience.
- Never use visualization just for decoration or to take up space.
- Be mindful of how visualization distorts the data, which is as unavoidable as distortion in writing about that data.
- Use color only when needed, and not colors that distract the eye or that are not easily distinguishable.

These formal rules could be easily mistaken for rules of classic prose composition, which counsels order, harmony, and balance, rules very similar to those of Edward Tufte, as explained below.

These rules also demonstrate that students, if given the opportunity, can think systematically and formally about visualization. The course demonstrated to me that these students—none of whom had any formal training in nor any expressed interest in art—can engage in metacognitive discussions of images, can discern high-quality from poorly designed images, can distinguish useful images from mere decoration, and can learn how to frame ideas visually. I am left to wonder: if visual skill were recognized as a core competency and given as much attention and status as verbal and mathematical skill, might more historians welcome the idea of visualization as an alternative to prose?

Definitions of Visualization

To reach this stage, historians would need to recognize that visualization involves much more than simply illustrating text or decorating a presentation in order to be attention-grabbing. By "visualization," I mean the organization of meaningful information in spatial form intended to further a systematic inquiry, what Elkins identifies as "information images" and Philip

Morrison calls "cognitive art."[10] I chose this definition to distinguish visualization from other forms of artistic expression—where inquiry is perhaps less of an issue—and from the larger flotsam of contemporary visual culture —where decoration is the main issue. Thus, visualization refers to a specific subset of all possible images; stated another way, not all visual images are visualizations. This definition of visualization derives from the sciences, which have a long history of "simplifying, abstracting, labeling, marking, and schematizing the chaotic phenomena of nature into orderly graphic form."[11] Like prose, visualization is a template for ideas, a means of ordering one's thoughts about a complex subject.

Visualizations may be categorized on a continuum between the representational and the abstract. Representational visualizations are pictures of the actual terrain and represent data that is already in visual form. Examples of these types of visualizations include architectural drawings and blueprints, which are pictures of actual or potential buildings and structures. Engineers use schematics in order to design prototypes; these schematics are then used in the construction process. Scientists use realistic illustrations to think about processes such as the water cycle. Geologists create images of strata. Our understanding of many natural processes has been helped by the images from time-lapse and slow-motion photography. Biologists rely on realistically rendered sketches of flora and fauna, as well as botanical classification drawings. Perhaps the best example of representational visualization are maps, both terrestrial and heavenly, which are pictures of a physical terrain. Surgeons and other medical practitioners employ images such as x rays, Magnetic Resonance Imaging (MRI), Position Emission Tomography (PET) and Computerized Axial Tomography (CAT) scans that may be thought of as "maps" of the human body. In each case, the image created is a picture of some portion of a visual field. I say "portion" because, like a map, representational visualizations are not the actual "terrain" being mapped. The "idea space," the environment in which the visual marks are arranged, reflects a selected portion of the actual terrain.

Abstract visualizations are perhaps the most intriguing forms of visual information, for as Stephen Eick sees it, this type of visualization is created via "a process of transforming data and information *that are not inherently spatial* into a visual form allowing the user to observe and understand the information."[12] As such, abstract visualization involves a translation procedure similar to the one that occurs when writing prose, where the writer converts data into a nonintuitively linear form. When we write, when we attempt to order chaotic data into some meaningful form, we are linearizing data that are not inherently linear. Abstract visualizations perform a similar service in spatial form.

For representational visualizations, creating an idea space usually involves cropping off a portion of a visual field. To make a map, an MRI scan, or a photograph means framing a portion of the "terrain" under consideration. In many abstract visualizations, however, the process of converting intuitively nonspatial data into spatial form means having to invent a "terrain" in which to place those data. Thus, an electrocardiogram (EKG) chart is an abstract picture of the rhythms of the heart, not an actual picture of the heart. A graph is an abstract picture of data in which the designer must first select the configuration of the idea space. When a table of numbers is translated into a pie chart, a bar graph, or a line graph, the designer is selecting a visual terrain in which to picture the data. Those choices—bar or line graph—are not trivial, for the choice of abstract terrain influences the shape of the data, thus influencing the representation of those data. To invent such visual displays means first having to design a space in which to place the information. In a way, abstract idea space is a type of visual metaphor.

Diagrams are a similar type of abstract pictures of data in which one must first choose an idea space. The periodic table of the elements, far from a mere illustration or decoration, is a spatial diagram that the chemist uses to order his thoughts about the properties of and relationships between elements. Further, chemists have used the periodic table as a tool of both discovery and invention. Given the organizational qualities of the diagram, chemists can speculate on the properties of elements not yet discovered or invented. The diagram offers a template for organizing research into these elements. It even allows chemists to contemplate the properties of elements that are physically impossible to produce. The periodic table is an abstraction, not an actual picture of a physical terrain. Consider all the different ways that the periodic table has been drawn, each reflecting a different type of idea space, demonstrating that such visualizations are constructions of the human mind, not pictures of an actual visual field.

Certain mathematicians contend that geometric shapes are also products of the human mind that, nevertheless, order our thoughts about meaningful concepts. For example, the mathematicians David and Gregory Chudnovsky have created three-dimensional images of pi in the hope of seeing patterns and structures in that complex constant.[13] As an abstract concept, pi has no intuitive form; mathematicians create such a form any time they write out the numbers, or draw a geometrical shape. The seemingly simple algorithm that forms the Mandelbrot set produces an exquisitely complex outcome that could only be appreciated once it was visualized. While visually stunning, the now famous Mandelbrot set demonstrates that visualization is about discovery and insight and is not merely attention-grabbing.

Scientists and mathematicians are not the only ones to use such abstract visualizations. A company's organizational chart is an example of how complex processes are given spatial form with a diagram. The organizational chart is neither decorative nor inconsequential, for it is often a regular feature of offices and cubicles in corporate life. For a business to function smoothly, one must be able to see the relationships between people, processes, and products. Change the visual shape of the organizational chart and a company begins to think differently about how it works.[14] Here is a case in which abstract visualizations allow one to order one's about complex phenomena.

Musical notation is another example of an abstract visualization. When a musician looks at a musical score, he is looking at an abstract picture of sound arranged within the idea space of the staff. Looked at in this way, a staff is a type of two-dimensional graph, "Europe's first graph," according to the historian Alfred Crosby. Like data points on a Cartesian grid, musical notes are arranged within an idea space that "measures time from left to right, and pitch according to position from top to bottom."[15] According to the music critic Edward Rothstein, the musical staff "gives pictoral representation of pitch, mapping out the high and low; it shows how different musical voices move against and through one another; it links the dimension of pitch and time, and gives image to rhythm."[16] Music historians contend that this organization of sound in two-dimensional space was a contributing factor in the emergence of polyphony, the complex interplay between upper and lower voices. Avant-garde composers such as Karl-Heinz Stockhausen and Brian Eno have explored new musical terrains in part by experimenting with the idea space of musical notation. Thus, the abstract visualization of a musical score is not simply a decorative illustration but a vehicle for communication, insight, and creativity.

As these examples illustrate, a visualization is distinguished from other types of images by its use. In each case, the visualization is not a decoration used to illustrate text or to make the information somehow more interesting and entertaining. Visualizations are not icons or clip art or cartoons. The creator devises the information image in order to organize, think about, and communicate ideas. We can identify a graphic display as a visualization if it invites the viewer to think about the information it organizes and if it generates new ideas or insights into that information. Rather than being a mere illustration, visualizations can convey meaningful information without the aid of prose. In fact, in an especially useful visualization, prose is unnecessary. Far from serving in a subordinate role to writing, the visualizations described above are meaningful conceptual tools of both inquiry and insight in their own right.

The Syntax and Aesthetics of Visualization

Examples such as the above remind us that when looking at any visualization—representational or abstract—we must not confuse the visual formalism with the concept being formalized. Like a writer of prose, a creator of a visualization must be mindful of the structural properties, syntactical and semantic rules, and stylistic conventions of the visualization. To those who believe images are simply decorations unable to convey meaningful information, the notion that visual composition has a grammar or some other formal structure might come as a surprise.

If writing involves the arrangement of words in linear order, then visualization involves the multidimensional arrangement of visual marks. Since the beginning of the last century, especially, there have been several attempts in a variety of disciplines to discover the underlying structure and formal rules of those marks—in other words, to discern a "language" of visualization. While what follows is not an exhaustive survey, it does point to the fact that visualization can be thought of in terms of formal rules of composition.

Linguists seeking to understand the building blocks of language look to the study of phonemes, morphemes, and lexemes. Those studying visual images seek similar building blocks of visual composition. Artists associated with the Bauhaus movement, such as Paul Klee, Gyorgy Kempes, and Laszlo Moholy-Nagy, were among the first in the twentieth century to identify a structure to visual language. Wassily Kandinsky also attempted to describe the underlying structure of images by breaking down visual communication into its constituent elements of points, lines, planes, and colors. Underlying all visual composition, he believed, was an abstract geometry of fundamental elements that could be formalized like any scientific discipline. "The progress won through systematic work," wrote Kandinsky, "will create an elementary dictionary which . . . will lead to a 'grammar' and, finally, to a theory of composition which will pass beyond the boundaries of the individual art expressions and become applicable to 'Art' as a whole."[17] Members of the Bauhaus wished to look beyond surface representation toward the "deep structure" of visual composition.[18]

Spurred on by the example set by the Bauhaus, artists and art theorists have been producing works that attempt to formalize the deep structure of images. One of the more popular of these works is the now classic text by Donis A. Dondis, *A Primer of Visual Literacy*. Like the Bauhaus designers to whom she is clearly indebted, Dondis breaks down visual images into the constituent elements of dot, line, shape, direction, tone, color, texture, scale and proportion, dimension, and motion. Dondis wrote this book as a pedagogical tool, to be used in visual composition classes to evoke in students an "educated understanding" of visual experience.[19] Such educated understanding of the visual is precisely what is missing from most educational experiences.

Dondis's primer parallels the Basic course taught by Bauhaus designers, which was intended to introduce students to the fundamentals of visual form and composition. Such a "Foundations" course is a common feature of schools of art and design. Students of graphic design often take such elementary courses as an introduction to their discipline; historians who wish to think through visual images may someday take similar courses as preparation for their own work.[20] It is not too far of a stretch to see "visual composition" as a required general education course comparable to "written composition," especially as visualization is recognized as a legitimate means of organizing information.

Semiotics is another discipline that has endeavored to formalize visual images. Fernande St.-Martin distinguishes two types of visual building blocks: open forms and closed forms. Open forms are various types of lines, distinguished by direction (i.e., unidirectional, bidirectional, multidirectional). Closed forms are lines that are joined together into shapes: regular or symmetrical, angular or curved. Jacques Bertin argues that any visual "mark" is structured by one or a combination of variables: shape, texture, value, color, size, and orientation. This example is notable in that Bertin looks to more than simply traditional high art and graphic design images. Bertin examines two-dimensional visualizations such as maps, diagrams, and charts.[21] Any formalization of images must be inclusive—that is, it must consider a wide domain of visual compositions.

Architects have also sought to understand the formal elements of their discipline. Christopher Alexander and his associates devised a "pattern language" that incorporated the study of architectural forms and urban landscapes. His "grammar" is divided into 253 "patterns" or recurring relationships between architectural elements. These patterns extend in a hierarchy of scale from the very small and intimate, such as a couple's bedroom, to the very large, such as the distribution of towns within a region. Designers and builders combine these patterns—for none exist in isolation—into networks of relations that produce satisfying living spaces.[22]

Beyond its significance for theories of architecture and urban design, Alexander's work is important to our deliberations for two reasons. First, his formalism deals with three-dimensional structures, as opposed to the largely two-dimensional formalisms of the Bauhaus and the semioticians (although their conclusions clearly have implications for three-dimensional thinking as well). Any effort to think visually must include a thoughtful understanding of the arrangement of elements in three dimensions, a consideration that a writer of prose never has to make, confined as she is to one dimension of representation. A three-dimensional idea space opens up another dimension of relationships between visual marks, allowing for a fuller network of connections. This leads to the second point; Alexander notes that the patterns in his "language" relate to each other as in a network, not a sequential chain. This insight is perhaps the most important element in visual thinking: that the syntax of visualization is far more complex than that of writing.

In the last chapter we divided written prose into two elements, words and syntax. I paid much attention to the formal properties of words, for words can often stand alone as bearers of meaning before they are lined up in written syntactical form. The elements described above—dots, lines, textures—cannot easily stand alone. That is, they have less meaning than words and in fact are more like phonemes. I believe a true understanding of visual formalisms comes through a careful study of the syntax of visualization, the arrangement of visual elements that produces meaning. If syntax is the root of language, then it stands to reason that syntax is crucial to understanding a "visual language" as well.

The syntax of writing is linear and one-dimensional. When we write, we arrange words into sequential order, in a line. Whether one writes in English, Chinese, or Arabic, words line up in a one-dimensional path. The syntax of visualization is not so confining. The elements of visualization identified above relate to each other in two and three dimensions; further, any one element might be linked to two or more additional elements. This is what Alexander means when he notes that his pattern language is ordered in a network, not a chain. Arranging data in this multidimensional manner opens up greater possibilities for picturing the complexities of thought and experience. For as the eighteenth-century scholar Albrecht von Haller noted, "Nature connects its genera in a network, not in a chain; whereas men can only follow chains, as they cannot present several things at once in their speech."[23]

The syntax of visualization thus allows greater freedom of arrangement. Rather than being confined to one dimension and one path of arrangement, the designer of a visualization is free to explore multiple and simultaneous arrangements between meaningful elements in two or three dimensions. We should also note, however, that because of this greater freedom of arrangement, visual syntax is also more difficult to formalize than written syntax.

Because of its multidimensional syntax, visualization can depict simultaneity more easily than prose. Often, in the chaos of actual experience, events and relationships occur simultaneously. Consider the following simple diagram[24] (Figure 2.1). With one look, we can discern the relative sizes of each of the shapes at the same time. When writing about these relationships, we must break up the simultaneity, for we must write "The square A is larger

Figure 2.1 **Simple Visualization**. This figure provides a sense of how the eye grasps visual information simultaneously and as a whole. Writing out the information in this diagram breaks up this structure of simultaneity and totality.

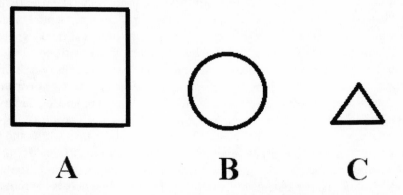

than the circle B, which is taller than the triangle C. Therefore, the square A is taller than triangle C." In writing out these relationships, we are forced to linearize what are essentially nonlinear and simultaneous phenomena.

This example demonstrates that relationships between data are often spatial, not linear. Many types of representational visualizations depict simultaneous, spatially ordered information. Circuit diagrams, schematics, blueprints, architectural drawings, and maps all order elements of information simultaneously and in multiple dimensions. We could describe the spatial information in these examples using prose, of course; however, prose would be unnecessarily cumbersome. If "a picture is worth a thousand words," it is usually because data are often in simultaneous relationships with other data. Think of a map. To write about the information in a map would mean breaking apart these multiple simultaneous relationships into one-dimensional lines: "Berlin is north of Milan and east of London and west of Moscow." It is easier, and closer to the reality of the situation, to look at the relationships in visual form rather than to write about them.

Simultaneous, multidimensional relationships are not confined to representational information. Data in an abstract visualization relate to each other in simultaneous fashion as well. The elements in the periodic table, for example, are arranged in such a manner. In addition to locating information about specific elements, the viewer can also group those elements with common physical and chemical properties, can compare the atomic weights and other properties of specific elements, and can speculate on the properties of elements yet to be discovered. In an organizational chart, one can see multiple, simultaneous relationships between different employees, their position in the hierarchy, and groups or clusters of work teams. Within the two-dimensional idea space of a musical staff, notes may be arranged not only next to each other but also on top of each other, to be played simultaneously. Unlike the one-dimensional syntax of prose, the harmony of music is a two-dimensional phenomenon. As my written descriptions of these examples indicate, prose linearizes what are essentially nonlinear relationships. Images more faithfully depict the complexities of these types of abstract information.

Well-composed visualizations thus allow the viewer to discern patterns in the data. An investor examining a time-series graph of a stock performance, for example, can look at the image and see patterns in the data that may not be apparent in a table of numbers or a written account. Lines of varying slope depict at a glance the rate of change in the numbers. When multiple line graphs are imposed on each other, visual comparisons between data can be made that are not easily detected in the words and numbers alone. Pie charts, maps, bar graphs, and organizational charts allow the viewer to see patterns of proportion, comparison, relationship, and process.[25] Cognitive scientists claim that the recognition of pattern in the midst of complexity is a telltale sign of intelligence; visualization provides one way of seeing pattern in data, an important requirement of any discipline, even history.

In maintaining the simultaneity that writing eliminates, visualizations allow the viewer to see the whole and the part at the same time. This might explain why it is easier in a visualization to discern holistic patterns and structure in the data. Consider the stock performance graph mentioned above. The investor can see both the price on a given day and the performance of the stock over a given period at the same time. When reading a block of text, it is more difficult—but not impossible—to leap back and forth between the whole and the part. "And unlike a page of writing," notes Donald Weismann, a visual image "reveals its subject matter in an instant . . . we are not required to follow any directional course from beginning to end in order to grasp its subject and be affected by its total form."[26] Perhaps this is one reason why computer professionals find visual information to be faster and more efficient than prose.

This ability to efficiently envision the whole suggests that visualizations are more conducive to synthesis than analysis. Synthesis involves the building up of parts in a system, of examining how the whole organizes the constituent parts, of how the "whole is greater than the parts." Visualizations, as Weismann noted, allow the viewer to grasp the whole with one look. Analysis, on the other hand, involves the breaking down of whole structures, to learn the intricate interconnections between the parts. Writing is especially useful for this form of thinking, in which the whole is less apparent than the constituent elements. One might define analysis, then, to mean "dismantling simultaneity" and synthesis as "envisioning patterns of simultaneity."

Visualizations are also an efficient way to see analogical patterns in data.

Analogy means drawing comparisons, finding resemblances and discovering similarities between two or more domains that, on the surface, appear to have no common connection. For the art historian Barbara Maria Stafford, "analogy is the vision of ordered relationships articulated as similarity-in-difference."[27] Perhaps more notably than writers, artists and image-makers have long used collage and assemblage techniques, for example, as a way to play with the mind's perceptual need to connect and find pattern even among disparate objects. Visualizations are a natural medium for analogical thinking, for the Gestalt principle of connectedness entices the mind to note common patterns, thus drawing associations and analogies.

This ability "to couple data that is not effectively or invariably coupled by causal laws"[28] is native to human intelligence, but quite problematic for those seeking to replicate the mind in the computer. Artificial intelligence researchers writing chess programs find it difficult to write code that allows the computer to recognize the resemblance of two different board positions.[29] Such "I've-seen-something-like-this-before" thinking is central to the way humans understand the world. Thus, far from being mere pop-psychological free-association, analogy appears to be an important function of the mind, an evocative means of seeking pattern in seemingly chaotic information.

While it appears that the designer of a visualization has greater freedom of arrangement and association than a writer of prose, not just *any* arrangement is permissible. An arrangement of visual elements must be meaningful and must conform to stylistic considerations. When I write a sentence, I am not able to simply line up words in any way I want. Sentences in fashion to this sense reader no written the make. (Sentences written in this fashion make no sense to the reader.) Chomskian linguists hold that we understand the proper order of words—their syntax—long before formal schooling, since we are hardwired to think syntactically. Perceptual psychologists similarly maintain that because of Gestalt principles, our minds seek out meaningful patterns in any visual field we look at.

Thus, as the information designer Robert Horn notes, simply juxtaposing visual elements does not a visual syntax make, just like the jumble of words above is not an example of proper English syntax. Although a designer might thoughtlessly arrange visual elements, "the Gestalt principle of connectedness urges us to make meaning out of connections between objects"; thus the viewer will seek out pattern even if no pattern were intended. Therefore, advises Horn, "we must be vigilant in visual language, perhaps more so than in prose, because [viewers] will attempt to make meaning out of elements whose proximity may be accidental."[30] This is not only because of Gestalt psychology but because the three-dimensional syntax of visualization is intrinsically more complex than written syntax, thus allowing greater freedom of choice with fewer recognized formal rules to limit such choices. Thus, an important factor in assessing any visualization is to carefully consider the quality of the arrangement, a point to which we will return in the next chapter.

Written prose involves more than simply the mechanics of grammar and syntax. As with prose, visualization must also involve stylistic considerations. Style manuals for historians typically advise classic prose formulations— that is, clear, simple, direct language as opposed to overly decorative, jargon-laden, or inaccessibly technical prose. It seems to me that if historians begin to think in terms of visualization, this "classic" sense will more than likely carry over into the new approach to history.

Perhaps the best style manual for "classic" visual composition is *The Visual Display of Quantitative Information* by Edward Tufte. Tufte contends that "excellence in statistical graphics [although his maxims apply to all visualizations, I believe] consists of complex ideas communicated with clarity, precision, and efficiency." His classic visual style consists of a few simple principles:

> (1) show the data; (2) induce the viewer to think about the substance rather than about methodology, graphic design, the technology of graphic production, or something else; (3) avoid distorting what the data have to say; (4) present as many numbers in a small space as possible; (5) encourage the eye to compare several pieces of data; (6) reveal the data at several levels of detail, from a broad overview to the fine structure; (7) serve a reasonably clear purpose; and 8) be closely integrated with the statistical and verbal descriptions of a data set.

Above all else, announces Tufte, "graphics reveal data."[31]

One way of ensuring that the data are revealed is for the designer to be mindful of the ratio between "data-ink" and the total amount of ink needed to construct the visualization.[32] "Data-ink" refers to any mark that carries the information content of the visualization. Other marks might be used to frame the data, like the x- and y-axes on a graph. These marks are included in the total ink, but not the data-ink. A person looking at a visualization of a game of chess, for example, should notice the arrangement of the pieces, not the appearance of the board.

Ideally, according to Tufte, the ratio between the two amounts should be 1.0—that is, all the markings in a visualization should be devoted to communicating data. Very few visualizations achieve this perfect balance, although Tufte identifies an electroencephalogram as a case where the data/ink ratio is 1.0. In most visualizations, the goal is to asymptotically approach the ideal through a process of revision and editing, minimizing non-data-ink and including as much data-ink as possible. The ideal visualization is dense with data, not decoration.

In unfortunate cases, the ratio between data-ink and non-data-ink approaches 0.0, since the visualization includes far too many decorative marks extraneous to the data. Tufte refers to these examples as "chartjunk,"[33] intentional and unintentional marks that distract the eye from the data. Tufte examines several cases in which designers allow the non-data-ink to overwhelm the visualization, as when the graphing frame and ticks overwhelm the data points and other marks that reveal the data. Unintended chartjunk includes moiré effects, produced when incompatible visual marks cause "strobing" and "vibrating" effects.

The most egregious cases of chartjunk occur when designers allow the graphic to be eye-catching rather than informative. Examined strictly from the perspective of the data/ink ratio, many graphics in school textbooks, business presentations, and publications such as *USA Today* obscure the data in color, technical virtuosity, clip art, and other distractions. When historians such as Alexander Stille dismiss visual displays as irrelevant and distracting, they might be referring to those overrun with chartjunk and very small data/ ink ratios.

Tufte's work reminds us that there is an aesthetic dimension to visualization. My definition of aesthetic here, however, does not mean "eye-catching" or "artistic," but refers instead to a satisfying performance within the rules of a certain domain in which one has a deep understanding. Such satisfying performances would include a brilliant move in chess, a great goal in soccer, or an elegant proof in mathematics, not just performances in art, music, or literature. Each is "beautiful," an aesthetic experience, satisfying to those who have an understanding of the domain in question. A soccer goal is beautiful only to those who have a deep appreciation of the game. The beauty of a move in chess is unfathomable to one not immersed in the nuances of that complex activity. Similarly, one who understands the rules of visual composition and syntax can appreciate the "beauty" of a visualization beyond superficial, eye-catching decoration.

Above all else, a visualization is beautiful when it is useful. A visualization is beautiful when it elegantly and appropriately makes the viewer think about the information organized in the visual display. A visualization is beautiful when it allows the viewer to gain insight and understanding into the information, especially when that information was not appreciated in some other form, such as written prose. A visualization is beautiful when the information is thoughtfully arranged in such a way that patterns and structures are revealed. A visualization is beautiful when it is appropriate, when the spatialization of information seems necessary and more appropriate than some other display. A visualization is beautiful when it is elegantly composed, when the graphic display does not call attention to itself, thus allowing the viewer to think about the information rather than the display. A visualization is beautiful when words are unnecessary to convey the information, or when words are needed only to illustrate the image. Far from being dichotomous, aesthetics and utility are joined together in a well-crafted visualization.

Translation Effects

There would be a major sea change in our profession if historians were to compose visualizations in addition to writing prose. Since the visual medium will free some of our thoughts that are constrained by written prose, thinking about the past in visual form will not be the same as thinking about the past in written form. Allowing visualizations to organize and constrain our thinking about the past would facilitate a different understanding of that past, in part because of the "translation effects" that occur when shifting from one medium to another. Where writing emphasizes sequence, unidimensionality, and linear chains, visualization enables simultaneity, structure, and association.

Whereas a written work of history emphasizes logical connections between concepts, a visual history might emphasize Gestalt-type connections that are not necessarily logical. The property of simultaneity inherent in visualizations might lead to a new sense of how cause and effect occur in the past. "Lining up" causes might no longer be a problem, for visual displays can depict simultaneous causes. Complex historic processes such as the Great Depression or the origins of World War I might be depicted as a network-like confluence rather than a linear chain.

Perhaps visual historians will abandon the goal of cause and effect altogether and instead seek visual analogy as the goal of their inquiries. "Like the crisscross, in Wittgenstein's *Philosophical Investigations,*" observes Stafford, "cross-cultural knowledge [of the type historians engage in] demands imaginative jumps through space and time to discover continuities and discontinuities with current events." Visual analogy "provides opportunities to travel back into history, to spring forward in time, to leap across continents."[34] Such a nonlinear leaping back and forth across space and time is counterintuitive to many historians, trained as we are to describe logical causal connections rather than picturing associations between disparate events. Visual historians might seek patterns of resemblance, not causal chains.

At the very least, nonlinearly leaping back and forth looking for analogies, simultaneity, and pattern might challenge the historian's traditional sense of chronology and periodization. Our preference for the linearization of the past is due in part to our understanding of time. Historians often champion diachrony—change through time.[35] Visual historians might instead seek to depict synchrony—events which occur simultaneously in time and space. Rather than writing about the stages of development in the past, visual historians might think about periodization as a mosaic of regions. Instead of a sequential time line, these historians might arrange events in two- and three-dimensional spaces: over there in that region are industrial societies, and over there in that region—parallel in time but not causally connected—is a largely agrarian society. In this visual depiction, the past begins to look like a topography of mountains, valleys, plateaus, and steppes, allowing the viewer to see disparate periods simultaneously. Like the shifting sands of the desert, changes in this structural topography of time seem directionless—that is, without linear progression. A belief in "progress" reflects chainlike diachronic thinking. Visual historians will have to dream up a new word that describes the changing configurations of structures in the three-dimensional space of the past.

Thinking in terms of networks might give historians a greater appreciation for synthesis and holistic structure over analysis and linear procession. Outside of the Annales school, historians have traditionally focused their attention on the narration of events, while sociologists and anthropologists have examined the larger, long-term structures of societies. As Louis Mink notes, the goal of the historian is to find the "grammar of events,"[36] suggesting that the medium of prose constrains us to describe a past that is linearly and sequentially "grammar-like." Historians employing visualization might instead use the new medium to depict holistic structures, the relatively stable relationships between elements in a system. Marc Bloch, Fernand Braudel, and other members of the Annales school were perhaps the greatest champions of holistic synthesis in history, since they wished to redefine history to encompass all disciplines—from geology to law to architecture—in order to describe the structural complexities of human civilizations as a whole. Historians often find such research agendas impractical and quixotic, for as Niall Ferguson has remarked, "without some kind of organizing principle, some hierarchy of importance, such history would be *unwritable*."[37]

Given the enormous scope of the Annales project, and given the communicative efficiency of visualizations, perhaps such a holistic structural history could instead be drawn. Something like Clifford Geertz's "thick description" could be translated into "thick depiction," where the historian visualizes an abstract, multidimensional network incorporating Annales-type social, cultural, economic, and political systems. A visual historian interested in comparative approaches might study "the iconography of structures," comparing and contrasting the visual patterns of different structures, such as the France of Louis XIV and the Japan of the Tokugawa Shogunate. Such a study would seek the visual resemblance and analogy in systems separated in time and/or space.

The structural properties of visualization will suggest alternative methodologies and historiographies to historians, a different way to think about the past. Surely, historians converting to a visual medium will retain many of the habits of mind that define written history, just as there are traditional historians who understand holistic thinking, simultaneity, and analogy. Likewise, visual historians might continue to think in terms better suited to the medium of prose. I continue to maintain, however, that the idiom of thought constrains and enables certain habits of mind that will make visual history as different from written history as the latter is from oral storytelling.

The accompanying chart is a simplification of this complex relationship. I offer this deliberate simplification to aid our thinking about the potential characteristics of the alternative practice of visual history.

Written history	Visual history
Logic	Analogy
Analysis	Synthesis
Chains	Networks
Causation	"Thick depiction"
Event	Structure
Diachronic	Synchronic
Linear	Nonlinear

As I indicated at the beginning of this chapter, these characteristics of visual history should not be viewed as "superior" to written history, only as an alternative. Visual history will be qualitatively and structurally different from written history.

Long before historians even approach the software needed to create visual history, however, we will have to develop an intuitive feel for visual syntax and aesthetics. We will have to become as unconsciously comfortable with the new medium as we are with the written word. For example, in the same way that the writer prepares several drafts of a composition before submitting it for publication, visual historians will have to prepare several sketches of a visualization. A sign that the historian has developed the intuition to visualize would be the presence of rough drawings, sketches of ideas, that are later "cleaned up" and clearly composed for presentation. Many an engineering design began as a sketch on a napkin at lunchtime; many an historical visualization will surely begin its life as a sketch, as a picture of an idea, as the following figures, drawn from my own sketches, illustrate (Figure 2.2).

Figure 2.2 **Examples of the Author's Preliminary Sketches of Historical Visualizations**. I have written articles based around an elaborate diagram, the written article serving as an extended caption of the visual information depicted in the diagram. Those diagrams usually begin as rough sketches like these. Just as when I am writing, I go through several drafts and revisions of the images. The diagram is never an add-on to enliven the text; the image is an integral part of the narrative or argument.

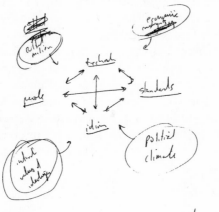

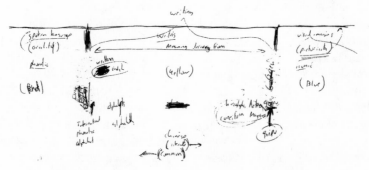

Acquiring this intuitive feel for visualization will happen only when our educational experiences change, when apprentice historians gain an "educated understanding" of visualization and visual thinking early in schooling. One "methods course" added to the menu of courses graduate students must labor thorough is insufficient; serious visual thinking will have to become a part of every student's general education, from elementary school onward, long before that student reaches graduate school. When looking at an applicant's GRE scores, admissions committees might look at the student's "visualization" score, not just the "verbal and quantitative" scores. In addition to a sample of writing, applicants might need to submit a visualization. Only then might history programs begin to draw from a pool that includes "image people" and not just "word people."

Before such a sea change can occur, however, historians would have to shake loose our collective distrust of images. Visualization will become an important part of our discipline only when historians allow images to organize and constrain our thinking, instead of serving only as a supplement to our words. Computers will become tools of historical visualization only when historians gain an aesthetic appreciation of the syntactic properties of visualization. In particular, historians will embrace visualization once they learn to view it not as a distraction but as a legitimate means of thinking about and communicating our understanding of the past.

Chapter Three

Visual Secondary Sources

An historical work is like a theatrical performance. In order to fully enjoy the event, theater patrons must suspend disbelief, that is, must understand that what they are looking at is not "real" but something that pretends to be real. Theater patrons know that what they are looking at is a set, not Elizabethan London or Neil Simon's New York. They know that the people in front of them are actors, not the people they claim to represent. The theatergoers understand that time and space on the stage are not real. Thus, several years may pass by in a two-hour performance, or the characters may pull the audience along between several places even though no one has physically left the building. Yet despite the unreality of the theater, theatergoers anticipate that they might gain some real understanding about human nature via the people, places, and events falsified on the stage.

We attend theater to be entertained, to be sure, but good theater also teaches us something useful about the human condition. Theater is a way to gain wisdom and insight, for while the characters may be made up, they reflect real circumstances. The playwright, director, set technicians, actors, and audience are all participants in a collective study of some facet of our reality. It would be ridiculously obvious—not to mention rude—for a skeptic to stand up in the middle of the performance and announce, "Well, none of this is real, you know. I mean, come on, these people are actors! It's not really an apartment in New York. And you expect me to believe that a whole day has passed between acts?!" Such a rude theatergoer misses the point entirely: we all know it is a fiction, but theater is a fiction that we willingly participate in, since theater is a type of useful fiction.

For a fiction to be "useful," it must have some meaningful value beyond mere entertainment. The useful fiction of a play is something like that of a scientific model. The physicist Freeman Dyson observes, "A model is a construction that describes a much simpler universe, [by] including some features of the actual universe and neglecting others."[1] Scientists rely on models even though they understand that the model is an abstraction of reality and not the reality itself. Consider the aphorism attributed to Alfred Korzybski: "The map is not the territory." Users of maps know that the object they hold before them is not the actual terrain they wish to traverse, but a model, a much simpler picture of that terrain. Since the only exact model of a system is the actual system itself, notes the economist Paul Krugman, "any smaller scale model of that system is therefore to some degree a falsification: it leaves out many aspects of reality." Nevertheless, that model is useful "if it succeeds in explaining or rationalizing some of what you see in the world in a way you might not have expected."[2] Thus, models, maps, and theatrical performances are "useful" if they generate insights.

A written secondary source is like a theatrical performance, or a model or a map. We know that when we read an historical work, we are looking at a "verbal model," not gazing at "the past." The past is long gone; all that remains are fragments, traces, scraps of memory that historians piece together, in order to construct useful fictions. In weaving together fragments of the past, historians engage in similar activities as mapmakers or playwrights or model builders: we create abstractions, we choose what to include and what to omit, and we arrange those choices into meaningful patterns. Thus, when I argue that secondary sources are fictions, I am not making a judgment about their accuracy—although some secondary sources are more accurate than others. Instead, I am pointing to the constructed nature of any work of history. Like all creators of useful fictions, historians arrange and juxtapose limited elements of reality in order to gain insight and understanding into that larger reality.

Secondary sources are useful fictions since they provide wisdom or insight into some facet of our past. To the ancient Greeks, "history" meant "inquiry," the disciplined interrogation of the past. "The job of the historian," wrote Louis Mink, "is not to reduplicate the lost world of the past but to ask questions and answer them."[3] Thus, it is the inquiry that matters most, the questions and answers and the benefits therein that historians seek, not the impossible task of resurrecting what is lost. It is pointless, then, to stand up and announce, like our rude theater patron, that an historical work is not "the past." At the same time, uncritical readers of history—those who look for the past to "come alive"—might need to be gently reminded that what they see before them is not the past, but an abstraction of that past.

While historians are becoming more comfortable with visual primary sources, they have yet to recognize visual secondary sources as useful fictions. All professional historians must produce a written secondary source—a dissertation, an article, a monograph—in order to be recognized by our guild. Without our recognizing them as such, visual secondary sources do exist in our profession in the form of diagrams, maps, films, dramatic re-creations, and museum displays. While these visual secondary sources surround us daily, historians accord them supplementary status to the "real history" we believe is written. If historians are going to use computers as tools for visualizing the past, we will first need to carefully consider these preexisting visual sources as models, guidelines, and standards.

Before that can happen, however, historians will have to recognize the value of a visual secondary source. Historians will have to learn to judge these sources not according to their entertainment value or whether or not they make the past "come to life," for visual history will need to serve as a scholarly inquiry for it to have any legitimacy in our profession. Like a written secondary source, a visual secondary source will have to be useful; that is, it will have to convey some wisdom or insight about the past. If "history" is to be successfully "translated" into a visual idiom, then its essence will have to be retained: the sense of inquiry, of interrogation, of questions seeking didactic answers.

Defining Primary and Secondary Sources

It might seem unnecessary to carefully define and distinguish between "primary" and "secondary" sources, for these are some of the very foundations of the historical discipline. That is all the more reason why we should thoughtfully consider these important terms, so that we might think more carefully about the usefulness of visual secondary sources. Note that what follows is a meditation on the formal structure of primary and secondary sources; I make no effort to discuss the accuracy or bias in the content of any source.

We are all aware that primary sources are artifacts produced during the period the historian wishes to study. What might be less obvious is how primary sources are created. All primary sources derive from a process that involves abstraction, selection, omission, and arrangement. Every primary source is an abstraction from the larger flow of human experience. Primary sources are objects plucked from the procession of events and fixed in some sort of material form.[4] These objects are one step removed from direct experience, for they are filtered through some idiom or medium. Like a color filter, which allows some light to pass while absorbing the others, the idiom filters out much of the experience, retaining some features which then make up the primary source. A letter, a photograph, or an architectural ruin are but written, visual, and spatial objects abstracted from experience. The primary source is a smaller part of a larger whole that nevertheless tells us something about that whole.

In abstracting human experience, primary sources reflect a type of arrangement. What we are left with when we hold a primary source is not the actual experience but rather something that has been subjected to a process. When one sets out to write an account, for example, some arrangement of the flux of experience is necessary. The writer determines what to include, what not to include, and the order of those events and observations. To see what I mean, try to write down your experiences today. You cannot possibly write down every event, every feeling, every utterance, for to do so would require more time than nature will allow in a twenty-four-hour period. When writing about an event, then, the writer cannot help but to arrange that event, by choosing what to include and what not to include.

As was noted in the first chapter, historians have long valued written documents as the most reliable types of primary sources. We assume that a written source provides more direct understanding of the period we wish to study. Professional historians can trace this preference for written documentation at least as far as Leopold von Ranke's insistence that legitimate history be composed from written primary sources stored in archives, those museums of written evidence. As important as Ranke was in establishing the foundations of the modern practice of history, our preference for written sources extends much further back than the nineteenth century. As the art historian Francis Haskell has observed, preference for written evidence dates to the Renaissance. While Greek and Roman historians were quite comfortable using art or other visual artifacts as evidence, "serious historians [since the Renaissance] showed themselves to be increasingly reluctant to use the evidence offered by art or artifacts when trying to interpret the past."[5] "Serious historians" relegated the study of images to "antiquarians" and have only recently begun to accept visual objects as legitimate primary sources.

We must not delude ourselves, however; written primary sources possess both the advantages and limitations inherent in the structure of any primary source. When reading a written transcription of a speech, for example, the historian is not directly experiencing the speech as the audience or speaker was, and is in fact missing much of what was originally surrounding the speech. The medium in which the source was composed—writing—filters out the reactions of the audience, the inflections in the speaker's voice, the qualities of the space, and the ebb and flow of the crowd. This is because the speech has been abstracted in written form, thus "blocking out" the nuances of speech, gesture, space, and movement. This rump experience is a compression of the actual event, a useful summary, a map but not the terrain. It includes and excludes elements of experience. Thus, when historians assert that only written sources capture the essence of past human experience, they must do so without illusion.

Written sources should not be singled out for these limitations. A photograph of the same event also abstracts from that experience, for the image does not convey the words, sounds, and movements of the experience. A photograph, on the other hand, allows us to pick up on the nuances of gesture and proxemics, the study of space, elements filtered out of a written account.[6] Like any primary source, the photo is a severe compression of the event, literally a single "frame" of an otherwise continuous experience. The photographer—consciously or unconsciously—arranged the source in deciding what to photograph, where to stand, how to arrange the people and objects in the shot, and when to click.

Thus, despite an historiographic tradition that teaches us otherwise, a written source is not necessarily "better" or "worse" than any other type of primary source. In fact, more and more historians are recognizing that a variety of primary sources aids in our recollections of the past.[7] Historians of ancient civilizations have long valued nonlinguistic sources, owing to the relative paucity of sources generally, written or otherwise. Historians working with non-Western, preliterate, or traditionally marginalized groups are also quite comfortable with visual sources. I found it odd when I switched my area of concentration from ancient to modern European history that visual sources were not more readily used. This attitude is changing, for the rest of the historical profession is becoming increasingly comfortable with visual primary sources. Will the profession similarly become comfortable with visual secondary sources?

For almost every historian, secondary sources are written. We have already discussed at length how the medium of the written word acts as a filter that shapes the form of the abstraction. As a linear idiom, writing imposes constraints on the type of secondary sources our inquiry into the past produces. As with primary sources, deciding to omit, include, and arrange is particularly important when considering secondary sources. The creator— writer, in this case—selects, discards, arranges, and juxtaposes primary sources in order to discern patterns in those sources. This arrangement and juxtaposition is neither random nor haphazard; the creator of a secondary source must combine primary sources in a meaningful manner, else no patterns emerge. Like Japanese *ikebana,* the "art" of a secondary source derives from the skill in arranging the sources. In evaluating such sources, then, we must consider the usefulness of the arrangement as much as the primary sources that are arranged.

In a written secondary source, the juxtaposition of primary sources is a crucial factor in the final product. The historian selects those portions of his sources that are most germane to his inquiry. Through chains of words, sentences, and paragraphs, he then joins these sources together. This act of joining, linking, and juxtaposing sources is the means by which the historian analyzes, interprets, and ultimately discerns meaningful patterns in the past.

Alter the order of the sources, jumble the relationship between those sources, and a different secondary source is created. Composing a secondary source is like sculpting: some sort of raw material—marble or primary sources—is fashioned by the designer's hands.

This process of juxtaposition takes several forms. The traditional monograph involves the greatest degree of overt arrangement and juxtaposition. But even an anthology or published collection of documents reflects a decision to arrange and juxtapose primary sources. The oral history collections of Studs Terkel appear to have very little comment or direct analysis by the arranger, so it would be easy to reject them as legitimate secondary sources. Yet Terkel has nevertheless organized, selected, arranged, and juxtaposed those interviews into patterns, a process that fits my definition of a secondary source.

Before we proceed, a word about "tertiary" sources. Historians do not typically make reference to such sources by name, although they make up an important part of the entire body of work in history. If a secondary source is an arrangement of primary sources, then a tertiary source is an arrangement of secondary sources. These take several forms. A bibliographic collection cannot properly be labeled a secondary work, since what is being manipulated are secondary works. Many excellent monographs in world history are tertiary sources, since the composer often compiles the account on the basis of secondary sources, not primary documents, for in a study so intrinsically large, no one could be expected to comb such a daunting collection of sources. Historiographic works are also tertiary, in that they juxtapose, inquire into, and seek patterns in secondary sources. This book, if I might be allowed the conceit, is a tertiary source.

In fact, it might also be desirable to think about the possibility of a quaternary source. This would be a juxtaposition of tertiary sources, the purpose of which would be to discern patterns in those sources.[8] Such a source would comment upon the work of those who comment on secondary works, which comment on primary sources, which are commentaries on direct experience. Theoretically, the process of abstracting and arranging sources could extend upward indefinitely.

I understand that the boundaries separating each type of source are not always so stark. A secondary work might become a primary source for an historian at a later date. A tertiary source might rely on primary as well as secondary sources. A secondary source might use other secondary works, thus reflecting tertiary elements. Any source that refers to the "literature of a field" ventures into the tertiary domain. Thus, in the actual composition of the source, a sentence or a phrase might send us leaping back and forth between many domains of inquiry. Having said this, it is still possible to label a source according to its prevailing pattern of source manipulation.

The designation "primary" or "secondary" refers to the level of the domain of inquiry beyond the original moment in the past. As I noted above, these domains theoretically extend infinitely. Whatever the level of inquiry, however, some sort of abstracting and arrangement is performed. Most historians work chiefly in the first or second levels, and occasionally in the third, and almost exclusively limit themselves to the idiom of words.

Visualizing History

While historians are recognizing the value of visual primary sources, they only grudgingly accept the value of visual secondary sources. At best, historians view these sources as "poor relations" to the real history we believe is written. At worst, historians are hostile toward any source that is not written. As was noted in the last chapter, some historians see visual secondary sources as nothing but inconsequential distractions.

Although historians generally distrust them, visual secondary sources nevertheless find their way into our professional lives. However, historians assume these sources to be supplements to written accounts, designed for the general public rather than a scholarly audience, and/or the work of nonprofessionals. For any of these reasons, we fail to accord visual models the status of "real history." If we were to remove these preexisting forms of visual display from the surrounding field of words, we might better understand their usefulness, not as mere distraction or pretty decorations that "grab the reader's attention" but as tools of historical inquiry. Further, a careful examination of these overlooked and misunderstood secondary sources reveals guidelines and standards for how historians might compose computerized visual secondary sources.

Below I briefly survey six types of representational and abstract visual secondary sources already in use by some historians: (1) galleries of images, (2) museums, (3) film, television and other moving images, (4) dramatic recreations, (5) maps and atlases, and (6) pictures of data. For each, I offer concrete examples drawn from history and other disciplines, where appropriate, noting their structural properties and limitations, and the usefulness of the inquiry afforded by each. My contention is that these "visual structures" are as useful as "verbal structures" in organizing our thoughts about the past and communicating these thoughts to other historians.

Gallery of Images

These are visual displays in which the spatial arrangement of visual primary sources takes precedence over the linguistic arrangement of written sources.

We are all familiar with the way that textbooks sprinkle their accounts with interesting photographs. Most of the time, historians display these objects as primary sources, for many of these sources feature a written caption that identifies the source, makes a comment or interpretation, and hints at ways the visual source relates to themes in the written account. In these cases, the visual source serves chiefly as a primary source, since it is isolated from and not arranged next to other visual sources. Placing a visual source within a written account is no different from placing a written source within the same account.[9]

Visual sources become secondary sources only when they are consciously arranged alongside other visual objects. These examples are fewer in number, but well worth the notice. For instance, curators at the Library of Congress have created *Eyes of the Nation: A Visual History of the United States*.[10] This is a collection of photographs, paintings, sketches, posters, motion picture stills, maps, and architectural drawings organized into historical periods. Alone, isolated within the pages of a text, these images are primary, not secondary sources. When placed alongside each other, however, they become part of a visual secondary source.

Recall that primary sources are the artifacts, while secondary sources are the arrangement of those artifacts. It would be easy to dismiss this carefully arranged collection of images as little more than a "scrapbook." One could argue that such a visual arrangement requires less "art" than a written arrangement of primary sources. However, as with a written secondary source, one must look carefully for evidence of the historian's syntactic choices, omissions, commissions, arrangements, and analytic effectiveness when assessing any visual secondary source.[11]

Effective galleries of images aim for some sort of association between the images. William McNeill, in his text *A World History*, includes "visual essays" in some of his chapters. These are collections of images that, when linked together, suggest visual analogies, in sections titled "The Radiation and Transformation of Greek Sculpture" or "Architecture in the Industrial Era." In one case, titled "The Mingling of Styles Eastward," McNeill juxtaposes four images of Buddhist statues from different times and different locations, asking the viewer to see the common stylistic traits between them as evidence of an ecumenical culture. While these images are helped along by useful written captions, the visual arrangement is clearly in the foreground, and the captions make up the background. Since McNeill is interested in tracking the changes influential civilizations exerted on their neighbors, visual sources "provide important clues to ancient relationships which the surviving (written) record sometimes disguises."[12] Yet these visual essays are not haphazard accumulations of primary artifacts; these essays are secondary sources, for McNeill has juxtaposed a series of images in order to discern patterns in the past. Like composing a written secondary source, McNeill has abstracted and arranged his sources to create a secondary source.

To be a truly visual secondary source, the display would have to overwhelm the written captions. That is, the figure and ground relationship between words and images would have to be reversed: images become figure, words the ground. Few historical texts feature this type of visual secondary source. Yet historians can readily find models from other accounts. Three chapters in John Berger's *Ways of Seeing* are "visual essays." There are no words accompanying these chapters, only a collection of paintings arranged in such a manner that the viewer is invited to see patterns themselves. This is not a totally unmediated experience, however. Berger has still sifted through a number of sources, selected some and omitted others and arranged them in an order of his choosing. These visual essays, says Berger, "are intended to raise as many questions as the verbal essays,"[13] thus indicating that carefully arranged images can be a source of inquiry, a requirement for any "history." Thus, to repeat, simply displaying visual sources is not sufficient for status as a visual secondary source; there must be some sort of purposeful arrangement or juxtaposition of several such images.

I have experimented with visual essays in my own classes. I have allowed students, for example, to submit visual essays in lieu of a written account. In the same manner as a written essay, the students had to answer a question, research their topics, locate appropriate (visual) evidence, and arrange this evidence in a convincing fashion, just as in a written account. I had mixed success with this assignment; I was unable to completely abandon the written idiom myself, since I insisted that the students write a brief caption below each image. Thus, most students, through no fault of their own, submitted what amounted to a short written essay about visual sources, which is not really what I had in mind. The students for their part found the assignment more difficult than a written account, which surprised me, given their expressed preference for visual information over written. All in all, while I was encouraged by their research and their final decisions about which sources to include, I was disappointed with the quality of the arrangement of those sources.

Working with a student on an independent study project, I sought to improve my own understanding of the issue of arrangement. This time, I instructed the student to compose a visual essay without the use of words in order to address some historical question. The student chose to explore the issue of racism in American history and used collage techniques as his way to answer my question. He took images from the antebellum South, the civil rights movement, and contemporary magazines, pasted them together, and showed (convincingly) analogous patterns of racism in American history across time and space. This was a breakthrough. The student's success proved that he understood that an important element of any visual secondary source was the "syntax," the placement of two or more images meaningfully next to each other.

Historians might well begin to investigate the use of collage techniques to uncover and display patterns in the past. In his interesting book *Metapatterns,* Tyler Volk uses collages in order to seek out visual analogies across space, time, and scale. A "metapattern" for Volk "is a pattern so wide-flung that it appears throughout the spectrum of reality: in clouds, rivers, and planets; in cells, organisms, and ecosystems; in art, architecture, and politics."[14] So, for example, in his chapter on "spheres," Volk constructs a collage that juxtaposes images from the myths and religions of cultures across time and space. In other chapters, Volk creates collages that display patterns across scales, from the microscopic to the macroscopic.

A collage is distinct from a visual essay in that the decision to juxtapose is more evident. Instead of "lining up" images as in a visual essay, a collage breaks down the white space between images, blending them together. Collages are not without limitations, however, as with any secondary source. Collages, for example, do not answer the question "why do these patterns exist?" They are better suited for synthesis than analysis. These collages do nevertheless serve a useful purpose: they are nontrivial ways to "compare and contrast" two or more objects simultaneously, creating visual patterns. Historians might try to redesign their texts so that images are arranged in order to see pattern, to compare and contrast across space, time, and scale.

Museums and Collections of Objects

Museums are similar to the images noted above, except that they are arrangements of both two-dimensional and three-dimensional visual objects. One of my favorite museums is the Campus Martius museum in Marietta, Ohio. One exhibit at the museum contains a collection of objects concerning rural to urban migration in Ohio.[15] The designers arranged the objects— ranging from maps and newspaper clippings to farm implements and household objects—into a narrative. That visual narrative is not haphazard, but is a deliberate arrangement of objects organized into paths through which viewers are invited to navigate.

Therefore, like the visual secondary sources described above, history museum displays are not merely artless collections of primary sources; the reconstruction of the past reflects a conscious arrangement of those objects into meaningful patterns, just as one might arrange the material when writing a monograph about the same sources.[16] Designing an exhibit is analogous to writing a book; curators, designers, and researchers must make compositional decisions regarding what to collect and what to ignore, where to place objects, the density of the objects in the space provided, and other issues of compositional style such as lighting and use of color.[17] The resulting display, of course, is not "the past" but an abstraction of that past.

Another display in the museum is the reconstruction of the Putnam House, the original dwelling of one of the first settler families in the Northwest Territories. In addition to preserving the original architecture, the house contains plates, cooking utensils, beds, and other furniture arranged in each of the appropriate rooms of the house. I especially like to walk around the fireplace in the kitchen, which is much larger than twenty-first-century versions and was used for decidedly different tasks, not as decoration but as the chief source for cooking and heating. I also note the lower ceilings and try to imagine the large Putnam family sharing such a small space.

I like walking through the site not so much for the interesting objects, however, but for the usefulness of the reconstruction as a secondary source. Look at the type of information we gain from this display. We learn something of the relationships between the objects, the context for those objects. By walking through the house, we learn something about the proxemics of frontier architecture, that is, how these settlers constructed and utilized space. We gain some understanding of building and architectural practices. This simultaneous experience, of course, could be translated into a written account. However, we would lose much information in the translation from the three-dimensional idiom to the one-dimensional idiom.

We must use such useful fictions with caution, however. Despite the tangible "reality" of the preserved house, the actual utensils and well-preserved spatial relations, it would be a mistake to conclude that this house "makes the past come alive." We will explore this idea in more detail below, but for now I would simply point out that this preserved portion of the past is surrounded by modern buildings, automobiles, electric fans, and contemporary clothing. Only a limited portion of the actual artifacts are displayed, either by conscious choice or lack of availability. The Putnam House, and any other form of historic preservation, for that matter, is a visual secondary source—an abstraction and arrangement of primary sources—and not the actual "past."

Thoughtfully placing three-dimensional objects next to each other creates a context that cannot be gained from viewing the object in isolation. Well-designed museum spaces arrange objects in order to create visual associations between the objects. Useful museum spaces include paintings, sculpture, and furniture from the period in question, allowing viewers to make associations between these objects that would not be visible if they were displayed alone. The associations evoked in these arrangements are simultaneous and multidimensional, central features of visual idioms.

Some historians disdain museums as too popular, not "serious" enough, or more appropriate to art than to history, despite the fact they are often created by serious historians. Part of the reason for this disdain might be that, as Gary Kulik notes, "the first professional historians had no interest in things. They were preoccupied with words," an attitude that persists among historians.[18] Yet we need not view a museum display as merely a collection of objects intended to entertain or commemorate, for their original function was to serve as a useful inquiry. In Western culture, museums trace their origins to the Kunstkammern, which enjoyed their heyday between the sixteenth and eighteenth centuries. Kunstkammern were literally "Cabinets of Art and Curiosities," collections of a wide range of objects such as natural materials, flora and fauna, and man-made objects. The stated intention of their creators was to collect as many objects from the natural world as possible; by displaying natural and man-made objects together, creators of Kunstkammern sought to narrate the evolution of the natural world, from *natura* to *ars*.[19]

Long before Kant defined "natural history" to mean the study of the temporal structure of the natural world, creators of Kunstkammern carried out this program. The Kunstkammern were intended as spaces that would bring order and systematic thought to the collected objects. Academics, and not simply disinterested aristocrats, found Kunstkammern useful for theoretical reflection, a model of the universe where the patterns of the natural world could be visually displayed.

Therefore, the idiom of thought in the Kunstkammern was visual and associative, not linguistic and logical. In placing objects alongside each other in a conscious manner, creators of Kunstkammern were not mere collectors; like the creators of collages, they were seeking patterns and associations between the objects. Thus, since their creators sought to inquire and not merely entertain, Kunstkammern were a type of visual secondary source. Given this background, then, historians might wish to look again at museums, not so much at the objects themselves or even the captions that provide the context for each object, but at the quality of the arrangement of those objects, and if that arrangement serves as a useful inquiry.

Film, Television, and Other Moving Images

Students are always demanding to see films and videos in my history classes, presumably because, unlike written accounts, videos "make the past come to life." If history were a séance and our goal really were to bring the dead back to life, movies would seem to serve that purpose well. However, history is a matter of inquiry, not séance. And films, videos, and television productions—

despite the appearance of living people—are still fictions, for they are all abstractions and arrangements of past events.

One of my favorite teachers made discerning use of videos in his classes. He selected representative cinema and documentaries and treated them with the same weight as the written texts. For example, when teaching about twentieth-century Germany, he showed *The Marriage of Maria Braun.* While the film is a metaphor of the economic miracle of the 1950s, my professor treated the film as a secondary source by examining how the director, Rainer Werner Fassbinder, made visual choices intended to comment on West German society in the 1970s, when the film was made. When screening such films, my professor would stop the action, discuss the images just presented, then rerun the film to allow students to see what they might have missed before. Thus, he accorded video images the same authority as a written text, and he expected students to be just as critical in assessing them (we also had to cite them in our essays). At no time, however, did he suggest that the film made the 1950s in Germany "come alive." Like a monograph, the film is a useful fiction composed in the 1970s about the 1950s.

When watching an historical film, it is all too easy to forget that what we are seeing is a fiction, a useful fiction perhaps, but a fiction nevertheless. This applies to documentaries as well as "historical dramas" like *Maria Braun.* Take, for example, the films of Ken Burns. His films can be classified as secondary sources since Burns goes through a similar process as an historian who writes a monograph. In films such as *The Civil War* and *Baseball,* Burns chooses which images to include (although his critics claim he is not choosy enough and needs to edit more). He decides on the arrangement of those images. He selects the words and sounds that will surround those images. More importantly, Burns attempts to inquire into his subject; for example, in the film *Baseball,* Burns shows that issues of money, greed, and the power of owners were as prevalent in the 1920s as they are in the era of free agents. Thus his film is not strictly a matter of nostalgia and commemoration, as are many documentaries. A film about the past is a constructed artifact and does not make the past "come to life" any more than a written text does.

When watching any historical documentary, we must judge whether what we are watching is a true "visual structure" and not just a verbal structure with visual illustrations. A good way to gauge this distinction is to listen to the narration while shielding the eyes from the images. In many documentaries, the words create a coherent narrative, as if we were reading the pages of a written account. Then, we can hit the mute button to drown out the words and determine if a narrative is created by the succession of images alone. Good filmmaking, notes the writer/director David Mamet, means carefully juxtaposing images in order to tell a story.[20] If the images in a documentary cannot stand alone as a type of visual narrative—something like a visual essay—then it is not a true visual secondary source. It is, instead, a "verbal structure" with visual accompaniment.

While similar to written texts, motion picture images are nevertheless constructed using different techniques, techniques unique to the medium. Historians recognize, however, that while the medium might enable certain fancy visually appealing techniques, those techniques must serve some sort of useful purpose. It does little good to have eye-catching displays at our disposal if we cannot make meaningful use of them. Like written accounts, films are useful when they enable us to inquire into the past.

Like a still image, the moving image depicts simultaneity not only of events but of idioms.[21] As a medium that displays many idioms, film is capable of depicting vision, sound, diction, gesture, and movement at the same time. Film provides a compelling way to depict much more of the Arnheimian "four-dimensionality of reality" than written words alone. Consider body language: just as people from the past spoke in different languages, they also moved their bodies differently, for every culture has its own traditions of movement. One can certainly write about movement and body language, but this information is easier to depict in a visual idiom. However, this property of the visual idiom should only be used when the historian truly desires to inquire into kinesic and visual elements of the past.

Films are also able to manipulate time, by speeding up or slowing down the action. In the film *Koyaanisqatsi,* Godfrey Reggio uses time-lapse images of downtown city traffic, creating a frenetic scene backed up by the pulsing rhythms of Philip Glass's minimalist score. The scene is certainly hypnotic and visually dazzling, but I also believe this technique is useful to the historian. By speeding up such scenes of human life, we are able to more clearly see patterns in what would ordinarily appear to be a chaotic and patternless event. Only when the film is sped up can we discern the ebb and flow of traffic patterns. What if we applied this technique to other human activities, such as crowd behavior or other venues involving the interactions of masses of people? Social historians would have an evocative analytic tool at their disposal. Thus, a film need not be mere entertainment or attention-grabbing, but can serve a useful analytic purpose.

Films also have limitations that need to be considered before they are welcomed as useful secondary sources. I have already noted some of these above, such as the fact that films are often confused with "real life." As Rosenstone argues, films are a poor medium for displaying generalizations or "social forces" such as revolution or industrialization, concepts easily depicted with words. By easily displaying individual people, films "personalize" the past, making film, for good or ill, more amenable to "Great Man" histories.

Rosenstone also notes that it is difficult, but not impossible, in film to display scholarly apparatus such as footnotes or bibliographies or the historiographic context of the work. Many documentaries, for example, do not pay enough attention to their "fictional" nature. Often, such films show images voiced over by historians or other experts who provide a seemingly definitive description of past events. Professional historians realize, however, that interpretations of past events are rarely so monolithic; we are always debating the meaning of those events. It might be more useful to have several historians commenting on any set of images, demonstrating the type of scholarly debate historians really engage in. Something resembling these scholarly conventions needs to be present in any film depiction of the past before we can confidently label it a useful fiction for historians. Perhaps only those advanced students who have been introduced to historiographic issues should be permitted to view films in a history class?

Dramatic Re-creations

I recently had the pleasure of watching an entertaining game of baseball played according to 1860s rules. The game was played by two teams of men dressed in period clothing, on an irregular field (the trees in the middle of the field were in play as was the barn in right field) with underhanded pitches and one-bounce outs. In addition to being entertaining, however, this re-creation of a common event from the past was also a useful way to learn something about the context of baseball over a century ago. I reflected upon what I was learning by seeing the game, about the multidimensional, simultaneous information that I am only dimly able to convey to you in words. Dramatic re-creations are something like films, something like museum displays.

Like those visual secondary sources, dramatic re-creations attempt to reconstruct the four-dimensionality of the past. For example, Chautauqua presentations seek to surround the written words of historical characters with visual information such as costumes. In theory, a useful Chautauqua presentation would include a careful study of how the person moved, including body language and gestures, simultaneous information too easily linearized in a written account.

Similarly, Civil War reenactment societies seek to re-create the sounds, smells, simultaneous action, and visual spectacle that was nineteenth-century military conflict. These multidimensional experiences are linearized in written accounts, leading to the charge that texts cannot make the past "come to life" as well as these reconstructions. Some of these reenactors are so convinced they can perfectly resurrect the multidimensionality of the past that they will go on crash diets in order to look like emaciated soldiers, or subsist only on meager rations, or wear wool uniforms in unbearable heat.[22] This is a well-intentioned, if somewhat extreme example of the myth that if one is diligent enough, one can make the past come to life. Like a method actor, these re-creators attempt to "feel" the past, experience it as closely as the original participants did. While military reenactments do include much of the experience of the four-dimensional simultaneity of reality, the participants and audience must remember that such reenactments are constructed "fictions" of the past, as abstract as a written account.

In some re-creations, the audience does not passively observe but actively engages in the fiction. Outside Indianapolis, a living museum allows the audience to participate in a re-creation of the underground railroad. The audience portrays runaway slaves, who are chased, caught, and verbally abused by slave catchers, allowing the visitor to viscerally "see" and "feel" the emotions of the slaves. Unlike a Civil War reenactment group, the audience at this performance is "immersed" in the fiction, like a theatergoer invited to interact with the characters on the set. But like a theatrical performance, these visual secondary sources are illusions, and thoughtful viewers must remember that what they are experiencing is not the past but a very good model of that past.

Dramatic re-creations are structurally similar to written secondary sources. While they appear to use more "concrete" examples, these sources involve abstracting, in that they employ visual idioms. Any idiom necessarily filters the experiences of the past. Thus even if we are "seeing" a man being shot, that visual experience filters a portion of the real event. As such, reconstructions omit a great deal of that experience, even in a well-researched drama. The organizers of such events necessarily make choices, as does any composer of a written account. Seemingly concrete visual performances remain exercises in abstraction and arrangement.

Further, re-creations can only re-create a small portion of the four-dimensional reality they attempt to model. In the same way a written account "leaves out" enormous portions of the total experience, dramatic re-creations leave out whole vistas of experience that cannot be captured in a visual image or well-made costume. These visual spectacles usefully display the "exterior" moments of historical events but are less useful in conveying inner thoughts and feelings, which written accounts, like letters and diaries, do quite well. Moreover, like a written account, a visual secondary source that attempts to model such a vast realm as "four-dimensional simultaneity" cannot possibly represent all the potential information. There can be no exact one-to-one correspondence between the model and what is being modeled, since not all the information can be preserved.

While re-creations, museums, and films are able to capture more dimensions of the past beyond what is written, at the same time they suffer from even larger gaps in what is lost, for these sources, like all sources, are composed from incomplete information. Thus, viewers need to be aware of not only what is visibly present but also what is omitted in any multidimensional visual secondary source—although this advice works as well for two-dimensional images and for written works, for that matter. Recognizing what is omitted in addition to what is included is like appreciating the relationship between figure and ground in a painting or between the white space and the brush strokes in Chinese calligraphy. Any secondary source is a dynamic tension between positive and negative information. I am not suggesting that every secondary source has to include every bit of information to be useful, only that our appreciation of the arrangement is enhanced by such considerations.

Maps and Atlases

Historians accept maps and atlases as visual secondary sources more readily than any other type. Although historians typically scoff at a visual display as mere decoration, we gladly point to maps when we want to locate events in space. Implicitly, we understand that maps are useful for conveying some types of information more efficiently than words. Thus, we are more likely to grant maps the status of "serious" history, if only as a reference work, something a "serious historian" consults or displays when writing does not suffice.

This close connection between history and geography has very deep roots, for there also seems to be a structural connection between historical writing and geographic mapping. The geographer Denis Wood hypothesizes that the impulse to write history and to draw maps sprang from the same source, namely the need for early civilizations to control their societies. "A variety of modes ranging from linguistic through the logographic to the purely pictorial," he postulates, "were used to record qualitative and quantitative information in both spatial and temporal dimensions." As these societies developed, the mediums of communication differentiated into forms recognizable today.

"*Temporally* ordered information . . . which was recorded using logographic and *linguistic means*," he believes "developed into what we recognize as writing (toward history and descriptive itineraries); whereas *spatially* ordered information . . . which was recorded using logographic and *pictorial means*, tended toward what we recognize as maps. Although these two traditions increasingly diverged, for numerous generations they were not readily distinguishable."[23] As history developed its criteria for serious research, distinct from that produced by antiquarians, geographers developed standards that distinguished them from early mapmakers. "Modern" maps after the Renaissance relied less on pictorial signs and more on abstract symbols, on verification through research and primary evidence, toward ends that we might tentatively describe as "scientific." When geography was professionalized in the nineteenth century, at about the same time as the professionalization of history, geographers developed similar rules governing evidence and scientific legitimacy.[24]

Because the two disciplines have developed so closely together, historians interested in visualizing history may well look to the geographer's map for their models. Maps are visual abstractions of primary sources, whether that be the topography of the Earth or the spatial relations between historical events. More importantly, maps are arrangements of this data; the cartographer makes as many choices about what to include and what not to include, and about the juxtaposition of those choices, as any writer of a monograph. Cartographers must decide what to map, which projections to employ, what types of symbols to use, and how to frame the map, a decision about which areas to include and which to "marginalize." As Wood observes, "The map's *effectiveness* is a consequence of [this] *selectivity*," for if the mapmaker did not make choices, the map would not be useful.[25]

Teaching this process of selection seems to me to be a useful skill often ignored in the training of an historian.[26] Keeping in mind that geography means "writing on the earth," I will often give my students a blank map and ask them to "depict the spread of the Black Death" or "draw the Industrial Revolution." Rather than memorizing place names, the students learn to visualize an historical process, select the types of symbols needed to convey the information, decide which elements of the primary information they will include and exclude, and thus create a useful secondary source that depicts historical events in space. These students need to be as careful in composing this visual secondary source as in writing any essay I assign.

Mapmakers engage in another level of this "art of arrangement" when they place several such maps next to each other, as in an atlas. The decision to group maps together chronologically or thematically is similar to the choices that a museum exhibit designer makes when deciding how to arrange objects or that a writer makes when composing a history. Moreover, the juxtaposition of maps in an atlas adds levels of meaning to the maps that are not present when the maps are displayed alone. A map depicting trade routes in the Roman Empire takes on new levels of meaning when displayed next to a map of the spread of Christianity.

Globalization does not appear so "revolutionary" when one juxtaposes a map showing British undersea cables during the height of the Pax Britannica and a map showing the distribution of cables that constitutes the fiber optic link around the globe [(FLAG), the network of underground and undersea cables that transmit digital information]. Viewers cannot help but to notice similarities, connections, and patterns that would not be easily detected if each of these maps were displayed separately, or in some other context. This juxtaposition, this syntactical choice, is the root of any historical inquiry.

Sometimes, the boundary between history and mapping is less clear, suggesting interesting possibilities for visual history. The Aztecs, for example, often recorded events in forms that one scholar describes as "cartographic histories." "The cartographic history," writes Elizabeth Hill Boone, "[very often depicts] simultaneity, spatial movement, and spatial relation at the expense of time."[27] In a written account of events, temporal sequence is the most important dimension of the experience, often at the expense of space. Thus, in Western histories, events are ordered by temporal markers: think of the notion of the "Jazz Age," a description of America in the 1920s. That experience, however, was not uniform in space. In Aztec cartographic histories, temporal events are depicted by visual direction markers, yet the unfolding of those events in space is the dominant dimension. In these accounts, therefore, time and space are depicted at the same time, although time is the ambiguous dimension.

One can find such cartographic histories in the West as well. One of the most famous examples is the chart of Charles Joseph Minard, who depicted the rise and fall of Napoleon's Grand Army as a wide line that moves in time as well as space (Figure 3.1). With this image, the viewer can watch the movement of the army, its location at any particular time, the temperature on the journey from Moscow, and the deaths of the troops along the way. J.F. Horrabin composed a striking diagram for H.G. Wells's *Outline of History* that depicts historical events in both time and space simultaneously.[28] The schematic was a type of coordinate system with time along one axis and geographic space along the other (Figure 3.2). Horrabin arranged symbols representing notable historical events within this framework. The growth of the Roman Empire, for example, was depicted as a steadily expanding area, an irregular shape that extends both through time and space. Simultaneous to this growing area are other peoples and civilizations—for example, the Huns. Their movement through space and time is depicted as a line. This line is deflected by a depiction of the Great Wall of China, located on the diagram at the appropriate coordinates (China, 220 B.C.), which forces the line representing the Huns to move westward. As the line drifts westward, it eventually pierces the large area representing the Roman Empire, taking a chunk out of the area. My written description is but a very small part of this complex visualization; Horrabin's visualization allows one to perceive simultaneously the whole structure and the individual events, in a manner reminiscent of a map or the periodic table. Like these other visualizations, Horrabin's diagram is not simply an illustration designed to break up or enliven written text: it can stand alone as a vehicle of historical thought and scholarly

Figure 3.1 **Charles Joseph Minard's Diagram of Napoleon's March to Moscow: The War of 1812.**
Minard's diagram shows several dimensions of information at once. The lines show the direction the army traveled, the width of the line shows the number of soldiers at any point, and the chart at the bottom shows the temperature on the trek leaving Moscow. This information could be written out, of course, but note how the eye sees the relationship between the whole and the parts simultaneously.

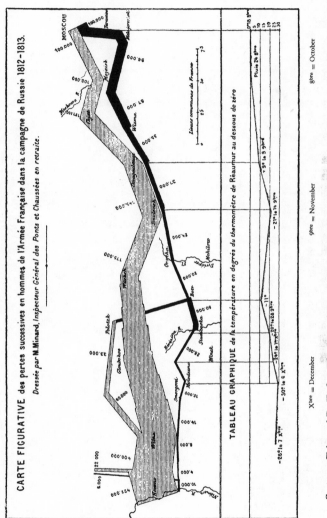

Source: Edward R. Tufte, *The Visual Display of Quantitative Information* (Cheshire, CT: Graphics Press, 1983), 41. Reprinted with permission.

Figure 3.2 **Diagram of the Roman Empire.** This schematic is a type of coordinate system with time along one axis and geographic space along the other. The growth of the Roman Empire is depicted as a steadily expanding area, an irregular shape that extends both through time and space. The movement of the Huns through space and time is depicted as a line. This line is deflected by a depiction of the Great Wall of China, located on the diagram at the appropriate coordinates, which forces the line representing the Huns to move westward. As the line drifts westward, it eventually pierces the large area representing the Roman Empire, taking a chunk out of the area. Imagine redrawing this diagram in a three-dimensional digital environment. Imagine a three-dimensional version of this diagram as a virtual reality display.

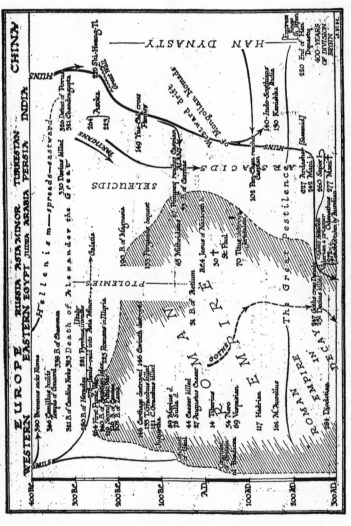

Source: H.G. Wells, *The Outline of History*, 3d ed. (New York: Macmillan, 1921), 1123.

communication. Like the directional markers in the Aztec cartographic history, the diagrams of Minard and Horrabin are ambiguous maplike objects that nevertheless display both time and space using a visual idiom. I imagine most professional historians would not define these objects as history, since the narration is largely spatial and maplike, not temporal and written.

While maps have certain advantages over the written word, we must also be aware of their limitations. Maps are excellent ways of displaying spatial information, but only the type of information that makes reference to the surface of the earth. All too often, this type of information is confined to events such as the growth of states or military adventures, economic life or demographic change. Eric Homberger has been "intrigued by the general difficulties of mapping certain kinds of historical experience. There are detailed maps of the battle of Midway, and of Pickett's charge at Gettysburg, but not of the changing configuration of domestic space."[29] What if one were to take the impulse to map—to display spatial relations between symbols which represent data—and apply it to historical experiences that are not tied to the surface of the earth. Would the resulting display continue to be a map? Or do we need to find another term to describe such useful fictions?

Pictures of Data

The science writer Stephen Hall maintains that since the middle of the last century, scientists have "completely stolen cartography from the purely terrestrial domain." They have redefined the idea of a "map" to refer to "a graphic representation of a milieu."[30] Thus, an MRI scan is a "map" of human tissue; astronomers "map" sections of the Milky Way; mathematicians "map" terrains of numbers. A map, according to this new definition, is no longer "geocentric," just about the territory. The boundary between a map and a diagram has been blurred. For purposes of my classification scheme of visual secondary sources, however, I refer to those visual pictures that rely on the surface of the earth as a "map." I define those images that display spatial relations between visual information without reference to the earth's surface as "pictures of data." These include diagrams, graphs, and other schemata.

Economic, demographic, and social historians have introduced quantitative sources into the practice of history. It is not uncommon for a monograph to include statistics relating to births, deaths, marriage, prices, wages, agricultural yields, industrial production, and other macrosocial data. These data are in fact secondary sources, for they are abstractions forged from primary sources. Numbers displayed in tabular or graphic form are not a surviving trace from the past. These displays are constructed artifacts made from parish and probate records, company ledgers, government documents, and other such primary sources. When the historian compiles these statistics in a form such as a table, we have left the realm of primary sources, for the historian has manipulated and arranged the remnants of primary experience.

Graph makers need to be as cautious as mapmakers. They also must make choices about inclusion, exclusion, juxtaposition, color, and symbols. In addition, a graph maker must "frame" the idea space of the data. All graphs need "reference lines," James Elkins's term for the "geometric lines that impose orientation and sometimes direction on an image."[31] Like a mapmaker who must decide on a projection, the graph maker must choose the dimensions of the x- and y-axis. Like a map projection, the choice of scale distorts the resulting picture of data; this distortion is an inescapable part of any graph. The slope of a line of numbers may be made to look sharp or flat depending on how the axes are drawn, thus affecting how the viewer understands the magnitude of any change in the numbers. The designer's choice of reference lines introduces distortions; viewers of graphs must keep this limitation in mind.

Graphs come in many geometric forms—pie charts, bar graphs, and line drawings—the choice subtly influencing the shape of the data to be pictured. For example, an interesting graph depicting total output during the Great Depression draws the information as a spiral, thus suggesting that world output was like water draining out of a basin. (Imagine the evocative power of such a graph drawn in three dimensions.) Graphs displaying industrialization are often drawn so that triumphant lines extend upward: more output, higher wages, higher energy use. These visual forms shape historical content and are similar to the linguistic modes of discourse identified by White.

Diagrams are even farther removed from maps, for if a map is about the terrain, then a diagram must first imagine a terrain. A mapmaker must make a host of decisions about how to compose a map; however, he must still ground his map in some location on the earth. Even if a map is not the territory, it is still *about* the territory. Graph makers are not bound by this geocentric constraint, yet they have limitations as well. By convention, most graphs are confined within a Cartesian space framed by coordinate geometry. A diagram maker must make similar choices, but because there are very few conventions governing the composition of diagrams, she must make an additional choice about the conceptual territory to be enclosed. Thus, not only must she create a "frame" within which to arrange symbols, she must also decide on what she is actually framing. In effect, the diagram maker must invent the territory. Designing a diagram is like playing a game in which the first move is to design the game board.

The time line is the most elementary diagram used in history. By "elementary," I mean that it is the simplest diagram we use, usually to help undergraduates and school kids to get the events straight before they can move on to more complex analysis. But "elementary" also connotes a fundamental principle. The time line is elementary in that it underlies many of our fundamental assumptions about the nature of time and our understanding of the past. Time lines are one-dimensional pictures of the procession of events. On a time line, time and events flow from left to right, like a sentence. Perhaps historians use time lines precisely for this reason: because they remind us of sentences.

Arranging time lines on top of each other introduces a second dimension to the visual source. This can be seen in the "Chart of World History," composed in the nineteenth century, updated at the end of the twentieth century, and marketed by a popular book store chain. Here time continues to flow left to right, but in this case many lines run in parallel, creating a two-dimensional display that can depict simultaneity, an important feature of any visualization. That second dimension is not clearly labeled, however; that is, there is no precise indication of what the second dimension represents. In some ways, it is merely an extended version of the first dimension, something like a fractal dimension of time.

However, some diagrams employ the second dimension as a way to depict space. Those visual displays by Minard and Horrabin would fall into this category, for they could just as easily be classified as diagrams, not as maps. To be more precise, these diagrams are not so much "time lines" as "time/space areas." Perhaps we could define these interesting visual secondary sources as ambiguous objects somewhere between a map and a diagram.

Less ambiguous examples of historical diagrams can be found in William McNeill's *The Rise of the West.* McNeill's designer, Bela Petheo, arranged symbols in order to depict the complex, abstract "terrain" of the past. After a cursory glance at these interesting creations, some historians might chortle at their cartoonish appearance, dismissing these diagrams as a less-than-serious inquiry into the past. However, if we were to concentrate instead on the form and structure of these diagrams, their usefulness and compositional sophistication become clearer.

We have already encountered "Japan, 1500–1650" in the introduction (see Figure I.1). Note how Petheo uses scale, icons, and two-dimensional simultaneity to depict the complex abstract terrain of the past. Note the different depictions of the emperor, especially his smaller size and lighter shading in the second panel, which is intended to show his change of status between the two periods. Note also how the overall composition conveys meaningful information. Petheo depicts the pre-Tokugawa period as chaotic, as shown in the actions and gestures of the characters, an apt depiction of this turbulent era. The other part of the diagram, the Tokugawa period, is calm and orderly, without the exaggerated movements and gestures of the first diagram, another interesting visual interpretation of the period. Once we expose the structural properties of these diagrams, we might better appreciate

Figure 3.3 **Diagram of Hammurabi's Society**. What is your eye drawn to as you view this image? We have been taught from a young age that we read from left to right, from the top of the page toward the bottom. When looking at images, however, our eye does not follow a conventional viewing path. While the eye takes in the whole, it then "zooms down" into the various parts of the diagram, then back to the whole. No two viewing paths are the same. As you view this image, and all the images in this book, make note of your eye movements.

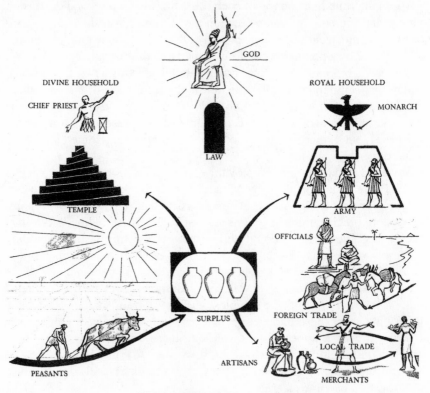

HAMMURABI'S GREAT SOCIETY

Source: William McNeill, *The Rise of the West: A History of the Human Community* (Chicago: University of Chicago Press, 1963), 57. Copyright 1963 by the University of Chicago. Reprinted with permission.

how these abstract pictures of data depict the past and how historians might employ them for serious scholarly thought and communication.

Petheo arranged symbols in order to depict the complex, abstract "terrain" of the past. For example, in the diagram "Hammurabi's Great Society," (Figure 3.3), the viewer sees simultaneously the relationships between royal and priestly authority, the economic and social relations between different classes, the hierarchical nature of the society, and its theocratic foundations. This diagram is more than a thoughtful arrangement of symbols; it is a display

Figure 3.4 **Diagram of the Evolution of Chinese Society**. In the first panel, the icon of the emperor dominates the scene, as he is depicted as much larger than the warlords and villages below him. He is also depicted as a military figure. In the Chou period, the emperor, while still riding his chariot, is much smaller and, notably, faded. The warlords are now much larger relative to the emperor and no longer connected by solid lines. Rather, the army (drawn from peasant households), the noble warlords, and the weaker emperor now stand in a looser relationship, reflective of the more feudal Chou period. The larger figures for the warlords reflect their de facto (and decentralized) control over Chinese territory, as opposed to the theoretical control exercised by the emperor. In the panel representing the Han period, the icon for the emperor has changed completely, from an active (albeit diminished) military figure to the more sedentary Son of Heaven, seated on his throne. Peasants continue to provide manpower for the army, but noble families now produce officials in service to the emperor's bureaucracy. Those noblemen are no longer depicted as warlords but as gentlemanly, introspective, scholarly, and Confucian. Direct lines return to link this system together, suggesting a more centralized, unified political structure.

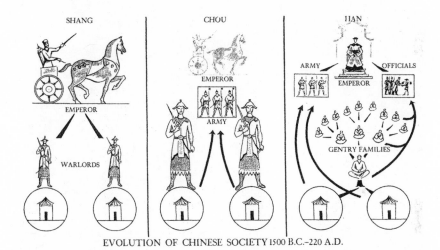

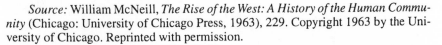

EVOLUTION OF CHINESE SOCIETY 1500 B.C.–220 A.D.

Source: William McNeill, *The Rise of the West: A History of the Human Community* (Chicago: University of Chicago Press, 1963), 229. Copyright 1963 by the University of Chicago. Reprinted with permission.

that maps out a terrain of social relations, a terrain imagined by the designer. This diagram, however, like a map, is *about* the terrain and should not be confused with the actual terrain.

The diagram titled "Evolution of Chinese Society" (Figure 3.4) demonstrates the thoughtful use of icons as carriers of meaningful historical information. Note how Petheo depicts the transformation of the role and position of the emperor in Chinese society. During the Shang period, the emperor is an overpowering military figure. During the Chou period, his status is reduced, which Petheo depicts by both his lighter shading and his smaller size relative to the previous depiction and relative to the army and warlords. During

Figure 3.5 **Writing Classification System As a Tree Diagram**. Historical linguists use tree diagrams as the standard way to depict the evolution of language and communications. Such a visual metaphor—a branching tree—suggests that, while different writing systems share common roots, they nevertheless sharply diverge from one another. I wrote an article—and drew a diagram—that challenged this visual assumption.

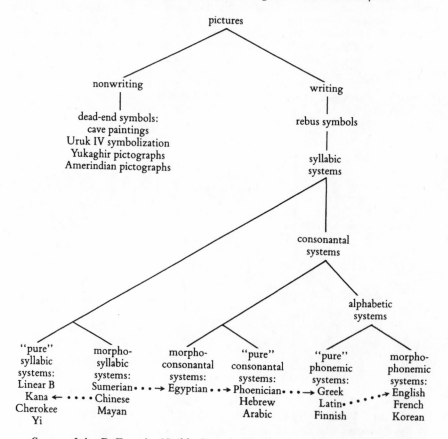

Source: John DeFrancis, *Visible Speech: The Diverse Oneness of Writing Systems* (Honolulu: University of Hawaii Press, 1989), 58. Reprinted with permission.

the Han period, the emperor's size remains reduced and the very icon for "emperor" has changed: over time, the emperor changes from a dynamic military leader to a sedentary, circumscribed Son of Heaven. Thus, in addition to two-dimensional simultaneity, the diagram employs scale, shading, and thoughtful use of icons to convey meaningful information.

The choices a diagram maker makes regarding the reference lines and geometric configurations of the "terrain" is an important historiographic decision. Just as a writer must decide on the questions that will shape his account, a diagram maker must decide on a geometric configuration that best

Figure 3.6 **Author's Writing Classification System As a Continuum**. In my article, I challenged the "visual historiography" of tree diagrams as a way to think about the relationship between various forms of communication. Instead of branching off from one another, I argued that different systems were related to each other as a continuum, with complex shades of difference between them. Writing systems sit in the conceptual space between language and image. The larger argument here was that communications systems are more alike than not alike. The diagram was not a way to break up the text; the diagram *was* the argument. The shape of a visualization and the visual choices therein are not inconsequential. (Note: the initial sketch for this diagram is in Figure 2.2.)

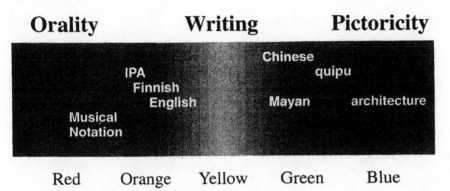

Source: David J. Staley, "Visualizing the Relationship between Speech, Image and Writing," *Comparative Civilizations Review* (Spring 1997): 86.

defines the shape of her account. New historiographic vistas open up when one challenges the geometric assumptions of a diagram maker. I once wrote an article that did just that.[32] In studies of the history and evolution of writing systems, historians often rely on tree diagrams. The geometry of these common diagrams asserts that as writing systems change through time, they grow apart from one another; the larger iconography of these diagrams is the triumph of alphabetic writing systems over all other forms of thought and communication (Figure 3.5).

My argument was that writing systems were more alike than not alike and that they are nestled in—not in opposition to—other forms of communication. In order to "see" this argument, I drew a new diagram not for decoration but as a useful object necessary for the inquiry. Tree diagrams emphasize divergence and distance; instead, I drew a diagram that placed writing and other forms of communication on a continuum, in order to emphasize the commonality, relationship, and wholeness of the forms of communication (Figure 3.6). Choosing the geometric configuration of the idea space was as important a decision as the arrangement of the symbols within that space.

The above example points to the fact that diagrams—and other visual secondary sources—belong within a visual historiographic tradition. In juxtaposing my diagram next to DeFrancis's for purposes of comparison, I was moving into the tertiary domain. When drawing or composing, visual historians are implicitly or explicitly placing their visual sources in relation to other such creations. Situating a monograph within the "literature of a field" is a common historiographic move; visual secondary sources can similarly be situated within the "images of the field." Thus, for a diagram to be truly useful, it must make some reference to this wider historiographic context.

Guidelines, Criteria, and Standards

The purpose of this brief survey of visual secondary sources was twofold. First, I wanted to note that visual secondary sources already exist in the practice of history. Historians, however, often overlook these interesting sources or relegate them to the status of distracting background noise. In this chapter, I wanted to bring these sources into sharper relief, to bring them into the foreground, to remove them from the surrounding fields of words that historians find more legitimate.

Second, I wanted to establish a set of guidelines drawn from these pre-existing forms of visual display that might serve as a heuristic to guide our thinking about computerized visual secondary sources. Before historians use computers as tools of visualization, they will have to develop rules governing composition, usefulness, and rigor. I can think of no better place to begin than our own practices, unexamined as they might be. I make no effort to discuss the accuracy, bias, or proper subject matter of such sources, only some rules describing the structure of visual secondary sources. What follows, then, are some rules of thumb for composing and evaluating visual secondary sources:

1. A visual secondary source is like a model or map or theatrical performance or written monograph. When properly composed, it is a useful juxtaposition of primary sources intended to inquire into the past.
2. To be useful, a visual secondary source must inquire, not commemorate or reminisce. It must organize the historian's thoughts and serve as a means of scholarly communication.
3. Visual secondary sources should not be used merely to entertain or to grab attention. Choosing to inquire in a visual medium means choosing to model a portion of the past best conveyed in a visual medium.
4. Any visual secondary source is an abstraction and arrangement of primary sources. Creators choose what to include and what to omit. Thus, any evaluation must consider the efficacy of the abstraction and the usefulness of the arrangement, in addition to the appropriateness of the primary sources chosen.

5. A visual secondary source is a dynamic tension between positive and negative information. The resulting source reflects evidence that is visibly present and evidence that is not present, either by choice or circumstance. Any evaluation of the arrangement should be informed by this consideration.

6. Often, visual secondary sources are analogical and associative, not logical. They allow the historian to see patterns in the (visual) evidence, allowing for comparison across time, space, and scale.

7. Despite their ability to represent more of the dimensions of reality, visual secondary sources remain constructed artifacts; they should not be confused with "the past" nor do they make the past "come alive" any more than a written account does. Even an "immersive" visual environment is a constructed fiction.

8. A visual secondary source, like a written source, should make some reference to its constructed nature. The creator should situate the visual source—implicitly or explicitly—within a larger historiographic context. Visual secondary sources should make reference to other secondary sources and should also identify a tertiary context.

9. Any visual secondary source must identify some sort of representational or abstract "territory." While the source is about the territory, it should not be mistaken for the territory.

10. Choosing the configuration of the idea space is as important a decision as the arrangement of the information within that space. Depending on the type of visual secondary source, the historian has varying degrees of freedom over the size, shape, and dimensions of the idea space.

11. Because the idea space of a display can be quite large or technically complex, visual secondary sources are sometimes collaborative efforts. In such cases, the person making design decisions plays an especially important role.

12. One must be aware of the limitations inherent in any visual secondary source.

Above all else, a visual secondary source is a structure that stands on its own as a carrier of historical information. Making a visual secondary source is not just a way to make illustrations. With these guidelines in mind, we may now begin the task of visualizing history with the help of the computer.

Chapter Four

Virtual Reality

One way adults have tried to convince children of the value of reading is by emphasizing its "virtual" properties. Children's television shows such as *Reading Rainbow* promote reading by extolling its virtues as an escape into an imaginary world. The introduction to that show features a cartoon image of a child opening a book as pirates, damsels in distress, dragons, and other fantastic creatures pour forth from the pages. In the children's book *The Pagemaster*, a young boy stumbles into an ordinary public library and falls into the pages of the books, where he meets characters such as Adventure, Horror, and Fantasy. Reading, so this familiar proverb goes, opens up the reader to worlds and experiences wholly different from our own.

Television and film have made this premise harder and harder to maintain, however, since children find it easier to immerse themselves in images of different worlds than to decipher words about them. The members of the MTV generation are accustomed to watching the images that accompany their favorite songs, rather than allowing the lyrics to conjure up such images for them. If our visual culture provides readily available imaginary worlds, educators and concerned adults might wish to seek some other, higher purpose for reading.

Computer games are the next in this long line of electronic media that promises to open up worlds for the young mind to explore. Computer games are not the same as movies or television, however. Since the graphics in computer games have become increasingly realistic and participatory, the young have found a medium that allows them to escape the mundane world and enter a fantasy world within which they feel invited to participate. Even television fails to entice viewers with this invitation to participate; why merely watch a football game when you can actually control the outcome of a game between two "real" teams? By contrast, reading words about other places now seems slow and lifeless. Thus, the old notion that "reading opens up the mind to different worlds" seems pale in comparison.

Computer games are a pop culture example of virtual reality. These are computer-generated, three-dimensional spaces with objects and people that seem very real and with whom viewers may interact as if they were real. Virtual reality systems have also been devised that allow the user to be surrounded by these images, as opposed to looking at a flat screen. Such immersive virtual reality includes important, nonentertainment applications such as flight simulations and medical simulations. Some observers, most notably Janet Murray, have speculated that these virtual reality environments will become the next site for narrative storytelling, stories having moved from oral epic, to novel, to film, and now to virtual environments.[1] While nothing like the Holodeck on *Star Trek*—where participants enter into a specially fitted room and interact with physically tangible objects and people—virtual reality offers the promise of transporting the viewer into "wholly different worlds."

Virtual reality holds great appeal to a visual culture brought up on movies, television, and video games, but will it appeal to historians? Members of this larger visual culture, I am convinced, will love "the past as virtual reality." Historians who wish to author virtual historical worlds will find an eager, appreciative audience. Accustomed to entering electronic virtual worlds, video gamers will no doubt be drawn into virtual Civil War battle sites or a virtual Roman Colosseum, participating as foot soldiers and gladiators. In the same way that they run away from narrative story in words, those raised in a virtual culture will eschew written narratives about the past and opt instead for virtual re-creations into which they will feel compelled to enter and participate. Will professional historians, however, be similarly moved?

The answer depends, of course, on whether or not historians insist on remaining strictly "word people." The answer also depends on whether the profession wants to make the "past come to life." Some historians have recently called for a "return to narrative." Rejecting jargon-laden, theoretical, and densely analytic prose, these historians have called for a return to "history as story," with real human beings and some sort of plot or moral purpose, as opposed to coldly scientific prose that seems to remove the flavor of human experience. This same "narrative" impulse might compel some visual historians to re-create the past through virtual reality technologies. Their re-creations—their virtual secondary sources—would be alive with real objects and real people with whom viewers could interact, rather than with abstractions to be monitored from a distance. Far from seeking merely an entertaining environment for video game players, these historians would instead seek to carry out the activities of the historian in virtual form: a scholarly inquiry intended to answer a problematic question, relying on primary sources, displayed as a three-dimensional virtual secondary source.

These visual historians and the consumers of their secondary sources will need to immerse themselves without illusion, however. Like any other secondary source, a virtual re-creation of a past event is a constructed artifact, not the actual past itself. There will still be a great deal of missing information that unsuspecting participants might easily overlook. Not all sources survive, nor can a virtual environment exactly replicate the "real reality" being modeled. Thus, despite what our senses might be telling us, a virtual re-creation is as abstract as a written narrative, only rather than being a model constructed from words it is constructed from three-dimensional images. Despite our best efforts, we can never hope to make the past truly "come to life." Virtual reality as a model for historical inquiry will certainly open up new vistas of interpretation, but it will be as limited as any other representation of the past.

Applications

While the word "virtual" is quite old, its digital connotations date to the 1960s. Computer scientists were already using the term "virtual" to connote "not physically existing as such but made by software to appear to do so from the point of view of the program or the user."[2] "Virtual" here did not mean simulated reality, however; it referred to the storage of memory in some form outside the physical hardware of the computer, as on a disk.

This meaning of the term was significantly altered by Ivan Sutherland. Already a pioneer in three-dimensional computer graphics, Sutherland, a computer scientist at MIT and later the University of Utah, developed one of the first virtual reality devices in the late 1960s. Dubbed "the ultimate display," it consisted of large, bulky, head-mounted goggles that projected images onto small mirrors in front of the eyes. Projected over the actual surroundings of the viewer, the images were little more than a simple cube that the viewer could observe from different angles.[3] Yet Sutherland proclaimed that the technology would lead to a three-dimensional imaginary world that not only looked real but felt real as well. "The ultimate display," he wrote in 1965,

> would, of course, be a room within which the computer can control the existence of matter. A chair displayed in such a room would be good enough to sit in. Handcuffs displayed in such a room would be confining, and a bullet displayed in such a room would be fatal. With appropriate programming such a display could literally be the wonderland into which Alice walked.[4]

Sutherland's work, which seemed impractical and esoteric, drew little attention at the time. The one exception was the military, which saw the benefits of these technologies as a flight simulation tool. Throughout the 1970s and into the early 1980s, the United States military as well as the space program invested in these computerized simulations.

Commercial application of virtual reality technologies became more commonplace in the middle of the 1980s. Although the term "virtual" had circled around computer science labs for decades, it was a former computer game programmer, Jaron Lanier, who first coined the term "virtual reality" to describe not only a specific set of three-dimensional graphics technologies but also the digital wonderland imagined by Sutherland. By the middle of the 1980s, the term was popularized in the mass media, and new applications outside of the military-industrial complex were developed, especially in entertainment. Virtual reality booths appeared at arcades and carnivals, where users donned goggles and fought imaginary battles.

Science fiction writers also popularized the concept of virtual reality. William Gibson, who coined the neologism "cyberspace," described a computer "matrix" in his book *Neuromancer,* where a user could "jack into" a computerized world by snapping an interface directly into the brain. Cyberpunk fiction writers prominently featured virtual reality themes. *Star Trek: The Next Generation,* the syndicated update of the 1960s show, featured the Holodeck, a virtual reality system that Sutherland himself would have recognized. Even outside of the relatively isolated world of science fiction, the term "virtual" was placed in front of just about everything, from "offices" to "sex," to describe a computer-mediated—albeit faux—experience.[5]

As this brief history illustrates, however, virtual reality is as much virtual as it is reality. The dreams of Sutherland and cyberpunk novelists are as important in shaping the debates about the applications for virtual reality as the existence of actual devices. Nothing like the Holodeck exists today. Despite real, tangible advances, the technology of virtual reality is still crude and clunky by those science fiction standards. No systems have yet been developed by which users enter a digital reality that is completely indistinguishable from actual experience. Even the realistic graphics of a video game are still not exact replicas of actual objects or people, and video game players know that they are still looking at a screen. Thus, advocates and designers of virtual reality technologies continue to think about applications in terms of both real and imagined potential.

While the Sutherland ideal is still far from actual reality, we might nevertheless confidently use the term "virtual reality" to describe current technologies and their applications. In my estimation, "virtual reality" describes graphics technologies with any one of three qualities. First, virtual reality systems must be "realistic," meaning either photographic realism or any variations on that theme, such as "surrealism" (real images placed in new or unexpected contexts). Second, virtual reality must be "immersive." Purists contend that the only true virtual reality is that in which the user cannot see a screen or the screen is large enough so that the user is surrounded by images. Thus, flight simulators employing giant screens or IMAX theater displays would qualify under this definition. Third, virtual reality must be "interactive." The viewer in a virtual reality environment is more than a passive observer. The viewer can manipulate the surrounding images, and his actions in that environment have consequences on the images that so surround him.

Current technologies exhibit one, some, or all of these qualities in varying degrees. None, however, approach the verisimilitude of Sutherland's wonderland. Although the graphics might be very real, they are not fully immersive; although immersive, the graphics are not realistic and do not respond to user movements in real time. Nevertheless, we might use the term "virtual reality" to mean the realistic rendering of objects, the ability of a user to interact with these objects, and/or the illusion of being surrounded by those objects.

While virtual reality has already been deployed in many fields, much of the promise of the technology is still speculative and potential. The entertainment field has been at the forefront of virtual reality graphics. Outside of the computer gaming sector, many Hollywood films feature computer-generated graphics that create realistically rendered spaces. Animation has undergone something of a renaissance with the development of graphics capabilities that make ordinary objects move around as if alive. These graphics also allow animators to "morph" people and objects from one form to another. Anyone watching television commercials, science fiction programs, or any of the many films generated from Hollywood each year is familiar with these applications.

Outside these mass market spectacles, serious artists have also begun to explore virtual reality as a legitimate medium, especially its interactive capabilities. The artist Toni Dove, for example, creates interactive virtual narratives. One installation, *Artificial Changelings,* is a large screen, surrounded by motion sensors, that creates a narrative space. By stepping on electronically connected pads on the floor, a viewer can move the video images forward or backward in time, thereby shifting the direction of the narrative. By moving her arms around, the viewer can influence the pace of the narrative; by standing still, she can make the sounds and visual images also stand still. The effect is like being able to influence the sequential flow of a movie rather than merely watching the screen. This installation suggests that virtual reality can enable artists to construct meaningful interactive visual narratives outside of mindless entertainment.[6]

Virtual reality has been deployed for training situations. As noted before, the military were among the first to use virtual reality, specifically as a flight simulation tool. The medical profession has begun to use the technology as a way for interns to practice complex medical techniques and for doctors to consult in virtual examination rooms and operating theaters. Air traffic controllers can gain "real" experiences of that hectic occupation before being given responsibility for real planes. In each case, the technology is used to simulate an activity that is too risky to perform with real people and expensive objects.

The technology is useful for simulation in less dangerous occupations as well. There appear to be many applications in science and technology, for example. Astronomers can create virtual models of planets, perhaps in preparation for landings. Engineers can test new designs in virtual wind tunnels. Manufacturers can, therefore, design, build, and test simulated products before committing large amounts of capital to actual construction. Chemists have wedded powerful microscopes with virtual reality technologies. The result is a virtual molecule that the scientist can manipulate and "explore" like an uncharted terrain. Such an approach to science sounds very much like the botanist Barbara McClintock's phrase "a feel for the organism"—that is, a level of intimacy with natural objects that yields new insights.

Architects are using virtual reality spaces to design and display their work. Rather than working strictly from flat blueprints, architects can now imagine and model their creations in three-dimensional space. Instead of wood and cardboard models, architects and their clients may now render and experience buildings as if they were actually constructed. Many a presentation now includes a virtual walk-through of the potential space for the benefit of clients. Revisions to the plan can be quickly adapted. While one may not be "immersed" in such environments, the realistic graphics allow for a certain amount of "virtual immersion."

Some users are deploying virtual reality to create abstract spaces as well. This application will be explored in the next chapter, but for now I wish to point out that some users are turning abstract data into virtual reality displays. In a sense, abstract graphs of numbers and spreadsheets of data can be "experienced" in three dimensions as if they were tangible, physical objects. There are fascinating implications of this application for certain types of historical narrative, which we also explore in the next chapter.

There are already several examples of representations of the past in virtual reality environments. Using the same graphics capabilities as professional architects, some users have modeled historical buildings or other architectural spaces. For example:

- Designers have created a virtual reconstruction of the sixteenth-century Dudley Castle in Dudley, England. The display, which uses a large screen projection system, was designed as a companion to a museum visitor's center. (See Figure 4.1.)
- Relying on engineering principles, surviving historical records, and the remaining ruins, scholars are reconstructing the market building at the Forum at Pompeii in a virtual reality space. (See Figure 4.2.)
- Researchers in Canada are reconstructing Canadian buildings long since razed. By examining fire insurance records, contemporary photographs, and other primary sources, these historians can digitally reconstruct and rebuild the nineteenth-century urban landscape. (See Figures 4.3.)
- Using Palladio's architectural design rules, students at the University of Waterloo have created models of "Possible Palladian Villas." The result is virtual Renaissance architecture that did not really exist—perhaps a type of "architectural counterfactual"?[7]
- Historians have developed a type of "interactive historical documentary" that reconstructs the second floor of the nineteenth-century Barnum's American Museum.[8]

The above examples are not exhaustive, only representative of the types of virtual historical structures designers are already creating for students and the general public alike.

It would not be too far a stretch to imagine an effort to reconstruct a virtual city in the past within which one could enjoy immersive interaction. The Foundation for the Hellenic World sponsors a "Shared Miletus" virtual simulation, where users can fly through a reconstruction of the ancient city, examining a wealth of architectural structures.[9] Using technology developed at the Electronic Visualization Lab (EVL) at the University of Illinois-Chicago, users need not be present at the same physical location to "share" the immersive experience. (Below we will examine the implications of this tool for scholarly communication.) The EVL has also helped to develop a "Virtual Harlem" interactive space.[10] Using a CAVE (a three-dimensional virtual reality system) environment, users can meet in the same virtual space regardless of location, something like a three-dimensional chat room. Designed to supplement a literature course on the Harlem Renaissance, the display allows users to walk through the streets of Harlem in the 1920s, with the option of listening to music. There are plans to eventually allow users to enter buildings, look into windows, and engage in conversations with historical characters. Imagine being able to walk the streets of Harlem and enter a building in order to hear Langston Hughes read a poem. These virtual tours clearly require a great deal of research into the primary evidence to re-create these scenes in detail, recognizing, of course,

Figure 4.1 **Virtual Reconstruction of the Great Hall at Dudley Castle**. Fill this space with computer-generated people and activity, then try to write out a description of the resulting tableau. Therein lies the potential value of virtual reality as a source of historical narrative. Imagine this as an immersive space, where a viewer could walk around and interact with people and objects.

Source: Computer reconstruction by Colin Johnson, exrenda.com. Reprinted with permission.

that as with any reconstruction there would be much missing information. These interactive displays are, therefore, interesting visual secondary sources: a useful way to organize primary source material.

Since the military has been an early advocate of virtual reality, and since video game manufacturers are drawn to battle scenes, it stands to reason that military historians would be attracted to the technology. The Pentagon, for example, used virtual reality to simulate battle conditions in preparation for the Gulf War. The next step would naturally seem to be the re-creation of famous battles from the past in the same type of environment. In addition to scenarios of future battles, historians could model historical battles, relying on the same primary source research methods that architectural historians use. The immersive and sensory capabilities of the technology would appear to be a natural medium for conveying the "face of battle."

Some historians have been drawn to the gaming qualities of virtual reality

Figure 4.2 **Virtual Reconstruction of the Market Building at the Forum at Pompeii.**

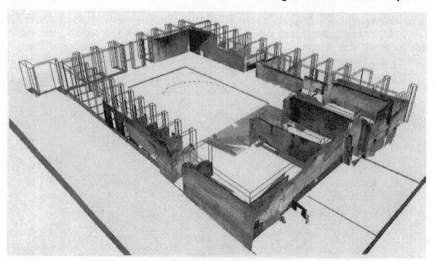

Source: Kirk Martini, "Pompeii Forum Project," jefferson.village.virginia.edu/
struct/pompeii/patterns/sec-00.html. Reprinted with permission.

modeling beyond the depiction of battle scenes. Historian Jeffrey Barlow
and his team at Pacific University have created a "game" in a three-dimensional visual environment.[11] The "game," called the Buddhist Palace (after
the software), is designed to introduce users to the study of Buddhism by
treating the stages of enlightenment as a quest or series of levels a participant
must work through. The Buddhist Palace is not immersive—viewers use a
screen—but viewers move through realistic renderings of Buddhist artifacts,
objects, and spaces, where they confront avatars who quiz them on various
points of Buddhist practice and history. I wrote "game" above in quotation
marks because, while the objective of the project is quite serious, the Buddhist Palace takes a narrative form that video game players would find quite
appealing. Young people who play video games will be immediately familiar
with the visual layout of this site and the idea of graduating through different
levels. Like Toni Dove's immersive narrative, Barlow's Buddhist Palace demonstrates that this technology can deal with serious historical content for
useful ends.

While the technologies involved are new, many of the above activities
sound very much like the kinds of activities some historians already perform. Historians working in museums, in historic preservation, and in ar-
chaeology already deal with the display of real objects. Almost every museum
exhibit is designed to be participatory: a space where viewers can interact
with the objects preserved. Thus I imagine that these subspecialties will be

Figure 4.3 **Virtual Reconstruction of a Portion of Nineteenth-Century Ottawa.**
This image from John Bonnett shows how historians can take primary sources, such
as photographs, maps, and fire insurance records, and reconstruct buildings that have
long since been razed. This process of reconstruction is identical to the work historians do all the time—doing research in the archives, weighing the evidence, piecing
together the larger picture. The only difference is that rather than writing up the results,
the historian "draws up" the results in three dimensions.

Source: National Research Council of Canada. Reprinted with permission.

immediately attracted to these new forms of display, reinforcing as they do
preexisting practices. As the above examples indicate, there are immediate
applications of virtual reality for teaching, museum work, and other ventures
aimed at the general public. The question remains: will the profession as a
whole embrace these tools and the modeling and simulation capabilities they
engender as legitimate products of research and scholarly communication?

Modeling and Simulation

All historians engage in modeling. As the historian Mary Webb notes, a model
is "any mental representation of an external phenomenon." Thus modeling
refers to "the formal representation of some aspect of a problem, idea or
system."[12] By this definition, every discipline employs some type of model,

whether physical models, like an architect's cardboard edifice; pictorial models, like diagrams; or mathematical models. Historians, in Webb's estimation, rely on "word models": representations of the past constructed out of words, sentences, and prose. Rather than creating one-dimensional linear models, historians working with virtual reality construct models in three-dimensional space.

Part of the training of any apprentice historian involves converting primary sources into a finished word model—that is, an article or monograph. Apprentices might also learn these methods by creating a virtual reality model. John Bonnett, one of the researchers working to rebuild virtual Canadian cities, contends that modeling is a useful pedagogical tool for teaching the process of historical thought. Students develop the habits of mind of an historian by locating and sifting through primary sources, determining which of those sources are the most reliable, comparing those with other reliable sources, and thus piecing together reasonably accurate information about the physical structures of the buildings, which can later be composed using computer modeling tools. That process—except for the last stage—is the historical method in miniature. Students fortunate enough to be taught history in this constructivist setting learn not only about the content of the past but the method by which the historian thinks about and reconstructs that past.[13]

Instead of a word model, however, the students construct a virtual reality model, a visual secondary source. The resulting model—while resembling an original primary source—is in fact a secondary source since it is a visual juxtaposition of primary sources. Like all secondary sources, it is twice removed from the reality it seeks to re-create. It is the product of a set of conscious choices by historians, a product of the selection, evaluation, arrangement, and juxtaposition of primary sources. Rather than being joined together by one-dimensional chains of words, these choices are represented in three-dimensional virtual reality space.

Like all secondary sources, the finished model is a balance of positive and negative information. In the finished model, there are omissions where primary source information does not exist. The historian must then weigh whether or not to make any visual inferences, a choice all historians make when they allow their word choice to fill in the gaps that sources don't reveal. But nothing in the final model is "made up" or fantasized. The structure is as faithful a re-creation as we can expect of any secondary source. Thus, a virtual reality model—before historians can label it a serious work of history—must be based on documentable and transparently available primary sources, not simply the imagination of the historian.

Virtual reality modeling, a legitimate tool of historical scholarship, resonates with many long-established methodological practices. But what is the value of the finished model so created? If it is in fact a secondary source, can a virtual reality model communicate ideas about the past? Like other types of models, a virtual reality model would provide historians a tool with which to communicate their "understanding" of the past. The economist Paul Krugman argues that any model is an imperfect representation of some real phenomenon that nevertheless serves as a tool for understanding:

> any kind of model—a physical model, a computer simulation, or a pencil-and-paper mathematical representation—amounts to pretty much the same kind of procedure. You make a set of clearly untrue simplifications to get the system down to something you can handle. . . . And the end result, if the model is a good one, is an improved insight into why the vastly more complex real system behaves the way it does.[14]

In creating a model, the historian simplifies the "vastly more complex real system" of the past into a form that we can then use to achieve understanding and insight about that past. In the above example, the mass of documentation Bonnett uses is then simplified into a virtual reality model. Krugman's definition sounds very similar to Max Weber's concept of an ideal type: a deliberate fiction that nevertheless offers some insight into a problematic subject. A virtual reality model, then, could similarly serve as a visual ideal type, a useful simplification of a complex real situation.

Very rarely do historians believe physical models and visual representations can serve as the final product of their research. Yet this is an acceptable practice in many subfields of historical research. Archaeologists and art historians reconstruct physical artifacts and design reconstructions of objects as the final model. A written article is, for all intents and purposes, an illustration of the visual model. The visual model serves as a tool of understanding, more useful than a purely verbal description. Similarly, creating a virtual reality model of a Civil War battle or ancient Miletus would allow for a certain understanding of those historical concepts. Like a film or dramatic re-creation, a virtual reality model maintains more of the three-dimensional simultaneity lost in one-dimensional word models.

Those who create models understand that the model is an imperfect replica. However, uninitiated viewers of virtual reality replicas might be enticed by the apparent verisimilitude of the display to conclude that the technology "brings the past to life." This is a dangerous fallacy. Any reconstruction—even the most realistic and sensorially spectacular—can never replicate the actual system being modeled, because of both the limitations inherent in any modeling technique and the missing information intrinsic to any secondary source, even a virtual reality model.[15] As with any historical model, not all evidence from the past exists, so gaps in the visual reconstruction will be unavoidable. The balance between positive and negative information basic to any secondary source might be lost on viewers overwhelmed by the positive information. Therefore, viewers will need to be reminded that a virtual reality model is as abstract as a word model, even if it relies on seemingly realistic and tangible objects. Anyone who witnesses a virtual reality model of the past will have to be instructed in how to use it. Like Magritte's painting of a pipe that reads "this is not a pipe," a virtual reality model should carry a warning label that reads "this is not the past."

In addition to realistic rendering, virtual reality models invite participatory simulation.[16] Rather than just creating models of buildings or realistic renderings of battle sites, virtual reality promises immersive simulation, allowing a user to "climb into" the model and interact with those objects, making the past seemingly "come to life." While model creation is an established part of the historical method, "participation in the model" is not as methodologically accepted.

One of the defining characteristics of historical scholarship—as opposed to mere antiquarianism—is that the historian endeavors to maintain an objective stance in relation to the past. Unlike anthropologists or sociologists—who cannot help but to interact with their subjects, try as they might—historians rarely have direct interaction with their subjects and the events they are studying. (There are, of course, exceptions, such as oral history projects.) Their interaction comes only through the remnants of that past as preserved in primary sources. As such, the historian is trained to separate "the past" and "history," in that the latter is a representation of the former. As a model creator, the historian learns to distinguish the model from the thing modeled.

Virtual reality makes this relationship problematic for the uninitiated viewer. One of the promises of virtual reality is that it is immersive; under ideal circumstances, viewers should forget that they are watching a digital display and should instead feel as if they are experiencing a real world. In the context of historical scholarship, this would suggest that the thing represented and the means of representation have become indistinguishable. The danger here is that in a virtual environment, the "past" and "history" would blur too easily, thus creating the illusion of a level of participation with the past that is simply not attainable.

That said, viewer immersion in a virtual reality model does possess certain attractive features that are legitimate elements of historical thinking. When a viewer "climbs into" a model created by an historian, that model has the potential to transform into a simulation. The interactive capacities of virtual reality allow a viewer to have some influence on the outcome of that simulation. For example, a viewer of a virtual ancient Miletus is presented with a myriad of choices about where to proceed. Will the participant remain high above the city, maintaining an Olympian vantage point from which to observe the city? Or will she fly down into the agora and interact with street vendors? Like a reader choosing the reading path in a hypertext, the viewer/participant in a virtual reality simulation chooses the "flight path" within a three-dimensional environment created by the simulation builder (the historian). "Shifting perspectives" is an important move in any historiographic debate; an historian who wishes to suggest a new interpretation of the sources often asks the reader to shift his "point-of-view." This shifting of views in a virtual simulation allows the viewer/participant a means of making historiographic choices usually reserved for the author/creator.

In so participating in a virtual simulation, the participant also gains a virtual "experience" of that event. While cognizant of the virtuality of that experience, a participant in a simulation might nevertheless acquire empathy for the past. Ranke counseled that the historian should understand the past "as it actually was." We could interpret this dictum to mean that the historian should try to gain a certain empathy with his subject: to cast off contemporary beliefs and assumptions in order to see the past through the eyes of those who lived it. Participating in a virtual reality simulation would seem to provide for this sort of Rankian empathy. Like a Civil War reenactment, a participant in a battle simulation would "experience" the past as did the actual soldiers. Like the viewer of ancient Miletus above, the Civil War participant would play an active role in the outcome of the simulation; through his interaction with virtual characters and simulated objects, his actions become an integrated part of the outcome of model. In such cases, the warning label I noted above would have to be especially prominent; participants need to be especially wary of the balance between the Rankean empathy enabled by the simulation and the critical objectivity demanded of historians.

Since a virtual reality simulation allows a participant the choice of determining the outcome of the simulation, it would appear on the surface that the participant serves as the "author" of the resulting "history." As Janet Murray contends, however, "There is a distinction between playing a creative role within an authored environment and having authorship of the environment itself."[17] While viewers in a virtual simulation may choose the direction and outcome of the history, these choices are limited to those designed by the creator of the simulation. Murray defines this second-order level of choice as "procedural authorship," which means

> writing the rules for the interactor's involvement, that is, the conditions under which things will happen in response to the participant's actions. It

means establishing the properties of the objects and potential objects in the virtual world and the formulas for how they will relate to one another. The procedural author creates not just a set of scenes but a world of narrative possibilities.[18]

In a virtual reality simulation, the historian is the procedural author. This role is very similar to the one played by museum exhibit designers. While viewers choose their own viewing paths, historians and designers construct all the *possible* paths those viewers might choose. Museum goers navigate through a space of objects arranged by the designer. Just as an historian pencils out several rough drafts of a prose composition, historians constructing a virtual reality environment need to sketch out these possible paths, using storyboards or other visual rough drafts. Thus, while viewers have great freedom of choice, their viewing path is circumscribed, one out of many paths authored by the historian.

Thus, a virtual simulation that allows participant control over the outcome does not imply that the historian is somehow irrelevant to the narrative. Quite the contrary: as the "meta-author" of the simulation, the historian has the ultimate level of control over the outcome. How will historians choose to use the power of procedural authorship? Despite the creative potential of this metalevel of narrative control, historians may not be comfortable allowing participants in a simulation the opportunity to choose the narrative path of the history, a role traditionally held by author/historians. It is entirely possible that historians authoring virtual simulations will so significantly restrict the choices of the participant that only one choice is really possible. These historians might decide to use the technology to create only one path, only one point of view from which the participant may interact. These historians might decide to treat the virtual reality simulation like a traditional prose narrative with only one possible outcome. The participant, then, would have only the illusion of making a narrative choice, since the simulation was authored to provide only one choice.

In such cases, the simulation would again revert back to the status of a habitable model; stated another way, a model becomes a simulation only when the viewer is permitted some degree of choice over the outcome. In a true simulation, the outcome is not determined. In a flight simulation, for example, the pilot can either land the plane successfully or can crash into the runway, with other outcomes in between. Depending on her choices, there is more than one outcome, each one equally plausible, the ultimate outcome far from predetermined. What if the outcome so chosen in an historical simulation is not one that "actually happened"? What if the historian allows participants in a Civil War reconstruction to make choices that allow the South to

win a decisive battle that it actually did not win? How many alternative outcomes are necessary in any simulation, and how is the historian to arrive at
these? Aside from the entertainment value, are there any legitimate scholarly
reasons to allow such an exploration of alternative outcomes?

The historian serving as the procedural author of an environment of choices
is like the writer of an historical fiction. In a good historical fiction, the setting, the context, the environment of the past is well established and accurate
even if the characters, events, and situations are made up. Wallace Stegner's
Angle of Repose nicely conveys the context of the nineteenth-century American West even if the people and events are fictitious. As the procedural author of an interactive virtual simulation, the historian similarly needs to be
mindful of the accuracy of the environment, even if the participant is allowed
to make historically "untrue" choices.

Procedural authoring of virtual reality spaces also requires a flexible understanding of causation. To envision multiple paths for viewers to choose,
historians need to imagine the unfolding of events "not as a single sequence
of events but as a multiform plot," which Murray defines as "a written or
dramatic narrative that presents a single situation or plotline in multiple versions, versions that would be mutually exclusive in our ordinary experience."[19]
Rather than one linear sequence, the historian who creates a virtual interactive simulation needs to think in terms of multiple outcomes, defining causation in the past not as a single deterministic line of events but as a number of
equally plausible alternative events. Like the psychohistory in Isaac Asimov's
science fiction novel *The Foundation,* virtual reality presents the past as nodes
of choices, forks in the road, moments when the flow of events could move in
either of two directions. To the procedural author, the past starts to look less
like a sentence and more like a flow chart: branching forks of "if . . . then"
choices that describe a number of plausible pasts. Historians usually refer to
this type of multiform "what if" narrative as "counterfactual history."

Unfortunately, historians tend to think of counterfactuals as merely a parlor game, not as a serious form of scholarly inquiry.[20] Niall Ferguson contends that the historian's insistence that history deal only with "what actually
happened" is deeply rooted in the history of our discipline. Whether one
believes history is guided along by Providence, Fortuna, the Invisible Hand,
class conflict, Progress, Reason, or simple linear cause and effect, determinism runs throughout Western historiography. While it is true that historians
have championed the notion of free will, historians generally tend to distrust
contingency and accident as an explanation for historical events. Therefore,
Ferguson believes, historians are not predisposed to examine alternatives to
the actual events, since any reasonable alternative would call into question
the determinacy so valued by historians.

Ferguson does not believe events to be so predetermined. He draws insights from twentieth-century science, especially the ideas of uncertainty, chaos theory, and nonlinear science. In fact, he includes history among those disciplines that study "stochastic behavior" (that is, patterned randomness). Ferguson evokes the concept of uncertainty as it pertains to quantum mechanics, which holds that the physicist "can only predict a number of possible outcomes for a particular observation and suggest which is more likely."[21] Because any physical system is exquisitely sensitive to initial conditions and because of the overwhelming number of variables which might determine the behavior of that system, it is not possible to predict the exact state of that system at any point in the future. One can only imagine a number of reasonable scenarios. If prediction is not possible, even for a physicist, how can historians claim to have uncovered the "single sequence of events" that produced "what actually happened" in history to the exclusion of all other reasonable alternatives?

A virtual simulation, therefore, need not serve merely as a high-tech parlor game: one should participate in such counterfactual simulations in order to gain a clearer understanding of causation in history. According to Ferguson, only when one understands that the procession of events is not governed by lawlike determinism and that events occur because of complex processes sensitive to initial conditions subject to many variables can the historian truly understand causation. "The historian," warns Ferguson, "who allows his knowledge [from hindsight] as to which of these outcomes subsequently happened to obliterate the other outcomes people regarded as plausible cannot hope to capture the past 'as it actually was.'"[22] Counterfactuals remind historians of the indeterminate nature of causation in the past.

Counterfactual thinking is not a license, however, to dream up *any* alternative. If this were the case, the number of possibilities would be so vast as to make any serious simulation impractical. Further, some alternatives are more possible than others; if a virtual reality simulation is to have any credibility, the procedural author has to be aware that some outcomes are anachronistic or unrealistic. Therefore, the historian must be mindful of limits on those possibilities in any simulation he might construct. It is important for the historian to make a distinction "between what did happen, what could have happened and what could not have happened"[23] when procedurally authoring a virtual reality simulation. The best way to accomplish this is to look for plausibilities rather than mere possibilities. "In short," notes Ferguson,

> by narrowing down the historical alternatives we consider to those which are *plausible*—and hence replacing the enigma of "chance" with the calculation of *probabilities*—we solve the dilemma of choosing between a

single deterministic past and an unmanageably infinite number of possible pasts. The counterfactual scenarios we therefore need to construct are not mere fantasy: they are simulations based on calculations about the relative probability of plausible outcomes in a chaotic world (hence "virtual history").[24]

Procedural authors of a virtual simulation would make narrative choices about which counterfactual variables to include in an environment of choices, rather than composing the one single thread of the plot as in a traditional written narrative. As the above discussion demonstrates, creating virtual models and converting them into immersive participatory simulations is not only a technical matter. The success and legitimacy of this approach ultimately depends on historians making specific historiographic and methodological choices.

History on the Holodeck

How well will traditional prose history "translate" into a virtual reality environment? Is there enough isomorphism between the two mediums or will some facets of history be unavoidably lost in translation? If so, which forms and types of history would be preserved and which might be forgotten? The virtual medium would appear to enable three general types of narrative form into which the prose of history might be translated.

The first narrative form I would label the "three-dimensional immersive collage." This refers to the arrangement of virtual objects in an abstract idea space through which a viewer might move. These virtual displays would resemble certain types of museum spaces. Some museum designers arrange objects in a nonrepresentational idea space in order to discern their abstract or conceptual connections, rather than attempting to re-create the actual context. Objects that might not have originally appeared in the same representational space are brought together in this abstract space in order to see conceptual connections. For example, sculptural depictions of the human form from a variety of places and times acquire new meanings and connotations when the historian takes them from their original contexts and places them alongside one another. These virtual museum displays would resemble the eighteenth-century Kunstkammern described in the last chapter. The creators of those spaces sought to arrange physical objects in an abstract space in order to explore their analogical and associative connections.

The same idea could be translated into virtual reality form. These secondary sources would be like habitable models, in that viewers would interact with realistic objects and could choose their own viewing path within the narrative limits imposed by the procedural author. The multidimensional syntactic connections between objects would be based on their abstract relations, not their actual relations in physical space. As in the Buddhist Palace described above, a viewer/participant would interact with realistic objects drawn from primary source research but placed by the procedural author into new contexts, revealing associations and analogies. The "history" in each display would be the arrangement of the objects, not just the objects themselves. History in this abstract idea space would reflect the concrete representation of concepts and ideas in nonrepresentational space.

A criticism of film as a medium of historical representation is that it cannot depict abstract concepts as readily as the written word because it deals in concrete images. Thinking of concepts and ideas as the arrangement of concrete objects in an abstract space might be one way for intellectual and cultural historians to explore new forms of narrative expression in the virtual reality medium. For any such translation to succeed, however, the historian needs to be able to depict concepts in some sort of concrete form, a process similar to a writer's quest to find "the perfect words" to describe some interesting concept. Clearly, not all ideas and concepts could be so depicted, in which case the historian interested in the immersive properties of virtual reality might be drawn to the "pictures of ideas" described in the next chapter. It is also possible that intellectual and cultural historians might eschew virtual reality as a form of representation, viewing the medium as incompatible with their interests.

A second form of narrative in virtual reality space is the "diachronic narrative." "Diachronic," which means "change through time," suggests the procession of events, usually toward some ultimate goal. As the technology currently stands, many virtual reality displays feature this sort of event-based diachronic structure. In many video games, for example, "The Quest" is the underlying trope of the narrative: the participant ascends through several levels in order to reach a final goal or outcome. While there may be several choices along the way—and indeed the skill of the player determines the outcome of the quest—ultimately the player wishes to arrive at some final destination that gives meaning to the entire game.[25]

Such a simulated environment appears to be teleological. For the pilot in the flight simulator, landing the plane remains the ultimate goal, even if she should crash along the way. The narrative here is structured as a series of events; the participant moves from one event to the next as she ascends the levels toward the goal. As these events occur and as the participant makes decisions, she would perceive the passage of time in the procession of those events and in the "if . . . then" choices she must make.

This type of narrative would seem to be appropriate for certain types of historical narrative. Military history would seem to be a natural fit. Participants would need to "take the hill" or "scatter the enemy's formation" or the more basic "win the battle, save the Union" in such a diachronic environment. Virtual diachronic narrative need not be confined to military history, however. In the previous chapter, I described a living museum where participants portray escaped slaves moving along the Underground Railroad. In a similar type of virtual reality simulation, participants would need to "find their way toward freedom" while making choices about finding safe lodging, avoiding slave catchers, and other such "if. . . then" decisions in an attempt to reach the final goal. Constructing such a virtual simulation would require the procedural author to write different plausible outcomes, as described at length above. The counterfactual method of thinking described there would be particularly necessary in these sorts of virtual diachronic narratives.

Diachronic narratives in virtual space might focus exclusively on the passage of time, even as the participant remains stationary. One of the benefits of virtual environments is the ability to alter the environment surrounding a viewer. In terms of historical narrative, an historian might procedurally author a space where the surroundings change through time. As in a novel by James Michener or Edward Rutherfurd, the viewer might begin in a muddy swamp, then watch as the swamp is drained, buildings emerge, and roads and aqueducts grow. The viewer would thus witness the birth of Rome from squalid beginnings to a grand imperial city without moving from the same "physical" spot. A student of mine once wrote a paper about the fall of the Roman Empire by imagining herself located in the province of Gaul and describing the changes such a hypothetical resident would perceive around her through time. In a virtual reality setting, one could stay in one place and experience the procession of time in such a diachronic narrative. The participant might also choose to change his stationary location and thus watch the fall of Rome from inside the city or at the imperial frontier. Further, the procedural author might grant the participant the ability to "speed time up" or move time backward, something like the character in H.G. Wells's *The Time Machine,* who manipulates the controls to watch time and events speed by him at a pace he determines. As with time-lapse photography, an individual could then "see" the movement of vast amounts of time, a privileged position unfortunately not granted to mere mortals. While not a direct participant, the viewer in such a virtual reality space would be permitted a high degree of historiographic choice by controlling both the narrative point of view and the pace of time.

A third type of virtual narrative is the "synchronic narrative."[26] In this form, time is not the chief variable of the narrative. Instead, the structure of human symbols, objects, and relations is the important variable. The viewer/participant enters this synchronic space not with a single goal in mind, nor is there any appreciable change in the overall structure of the space. Synchronic narratives are not event-driven but resemble a Braudelian narrative or Annales-type "thick depiction" of a three-dimensional historical space. In this sense, such a narrative seems more "anthropological" rather than traditionally "historical" since it emphasizes structure over event, stable relations over change through time.

The tour of ancient Miletus described above fits this description of a synchronic narrative. The "city" in this virtual environment remains a stable set of structures within which the participant may move and interact. The goal is not teleological; that is, the viewer need not attain some specific outcome, but instead gains understanding. A viewer would still make choices: do I go here or there? Do I want to see the city from above or in a particular location? What parts of the city would be denied to me, and how does this alter my understanding of the life of the city? In such a synchronic environment, scholarly possibilities abound. A participant could, for example, explore social spaces, such as the separate male and female spheres of the city. Thus, a synchronic space need not be simply an elaborate architectural model; it could be an environment where one could explore the symbolic relationships between people and objects that constitute social space.

In this narrative form, historians might readily translate social history into a virtual reality environment. A graduate teacher of mine once reminded us that for social history to be truly effective, the historian should be able to evoke and reconstruct the smells of his grandmother's kitchen. The social historian could procedurally author a synchronic narrative that could evoke that space (although perhaps without the smells). The medieval manor, the preindustrial household, the monastery, or the domestic spaces of 1950s suburbia could all be depicted in a synchronic virtual narrative. A participant moving through such spaces would gain the type of three-dimensional understanding about and empathy for these spaces that well-designed historical reconstructions and reenactments evoke.

As these examples indicate, virtual reality need not be dominated by military applications. The history of the technology suggests otherwise, however. The first applications of the technology were for military simulations. The entertainment sector has used virtual reality graphics to depict battle scenes and other violent and extreme images. As this technology has become more commonplace, some thoughtful critics have wondered whether or not virtual reality will continue to retain these masculine, misogynistic characteristics. The "plots" of many video games, for example, feature violent visual spectacles; as the artist Toni Dove observes, in the virtual environment as it currently stands, "Narrative strategies shift away from character- and plot-driven stories to experiences that escalate physical and visual intensities."[27] Because the technology seems so physical, tactile, and visually stimulating, there is every reason to believe that virtual reality will be used to create spectacles.

Does this mean that only the spectacles of the past will "translate" into virtual environments? If one believes that the medium can depict only visual spectacle, then it would appear that only the sensorially extreme events of the past—battles, riots, assassinations, book burnings—would be translated into virtual form. This would imply that only a selected portion of the past could be so translated; if the technology becomes an important medium for historical reconstructions, much of the past would be lost in translation.[28]

As my above examples indicate, however, the technology is not inherently masculine, violent, or sensorially extreme. These are, rather, choices made by designers and procedural authors, not a constraint of the technology. Virtual reality would seem to be more "real" and less abstract than a written text, but this need not mean a descent into visual spectacle. Historians are just as likely to re-create scenes of everyday life or immersive collages as they are the battle of Gettysburg. I have been emphasizing the three-dimensional qualities of the medium; that is, the ability to depict three-dimensional simultaneous structures that written prose linearizes. Historians could aply this property of the medium to any number of problems in the past, not just simply the extreme events.

As I noted above, there will be a ready, appreciative audience for this type of three-dimensional immersive visual history. Companies specializing in re-creations of historic spaces are already popping up on-line, and there is every reason to suspect that such firms will continue to represent the past in virtual space. The forms of history that finally emerge in the virtual environment will be determined by both the identity and qualifications of the procedural authors and the intentions and expectations of the audience. The issue, then, is not *if* virtual history will arrive but *whether* professional historians will be willing participants in this endeavor.

I imagine that, given the technological barriers to entry, capital-intensive companies will dominate the production of virtual reality history, at least in the short run. In an ideal world, professional historians would serve as the primary designers and procedural authors of the environment. It would be unrealistic, however, to assume that an historian could master all of the technical requirements to construct a virtual reality display alone. This would be like one person designing, contracting, and building a skyscraper. It would be more realistic to assume that the historian—as the procedural author—would serve as the "architect" of the virtual reality edifice, the one who conceives of and designs the structure that others construct. Unfortunately, it is just as likely that, as with many "historical" films researched by historians but ultimately designed by nonhistorians, historians working with virtual reality might simply play a supporting role as consulting members of a collaborative team directed by nonhistorians.

These companies will find ready-made audiences for their products. The same "general public" that watches Oliver Stone movies, attends museums and reenactments, and watches the History Channel would likely be very attracted to an immersive environment in which it could enjoy the illusion of participation in the past. Schoolchildren eager to have the past "come to life" would go on field trips "back into the past," rather than simply reading about it in the present.[29] Video gamers and others immersed in visual culture—usually more forward-looking and futuristic—might be "hooked into the past" by this technology. For those who find professional history too abstract, irrelevant, or disconnected from their own understanding of the past, the verisimilitude and concrete realism of a virtual immersive environment might invigorate interest in the past.

That "past," however, would not necessarily be "history." There is every reason to assume that companies that design such virtual environments would not include the warning label I noted above saying "This is not the past but a model of the past." Rather than participating in a simulation in order to engage in a useful inquiry, the goal of these displays—aside from money-making—might be to promote a type of "nostalgic entertainment" or, as noted above, "visual spectacle." Participants might be lured by the promise of agency and choice within a virtual environment, but concerns about procedural authorship and positive and negative information might be less of an issue.

Schoolteachers, wishing to find "interesting" ways of teaching history or to appeal to "visual learners," might uncritically accept these non-professionally produced simulations as legitimate history. The historian's understanding of the past might not be the one shared by those constructing and participating in virtual simulations.

I fear, therefore, that if virtual reality is designed by nonprofessionals and marketed to the general public as nostalgic entertainment or mere voyeuristic spectacle, these visual displays would have the same professional standing as museums and films currently do. That is, professional historians would view virtual reality as interesting, necessary for an uninitiated general public, but ultimately a watered-down type of history. Such a view would perpetuate the notion that serious history is written and popular history is visual. Some historians will no doubt wish to study virtual history as a professional vocation. Like historians who study film, they might write articles or reviews of interesting applications for professional journals. These historians might write critiques of virtual simulations, assessing the accuracy, the positive and negative information, and the quality of the model-building.

These historians would never dream of procedurally authoring their own virtual environment, however, for they would understand that such displays would be laughed at by "serious" historians—and never count toward tenure and promotion.

Only if the profession treats virtual displays with the same seriousness and legitimacy as it does written monographs could virtual reality serve as a tool of historical inquiry. This will come about only when historians employ the technology for useful inquiries and scholarly communication. That is, both the designers of and the audience for virtual history would have to be professional.

Imagine this scenario. An historian arrives at a conference with a new simulation of a medieval village. The procedural author of the simulation has created the virtual display as an expression of her understanding of the past being modeled. She knows that her simulation is a useful model: a simplification of a complex real system that nevertheless offers insight into and understanding of that real system. She has conducted primary source research, has weighed the authenticity of various forms of evidence, is aware of previous interpretations and larger historiographic issues. The procedural author has new evidence, drawn from archival research, that suggests new ways to understand gender roles in the medieval village. Her intention then is to explore the "gendered spaces" of the medieval village. The historian has procedurally authored a synchronic narrative of that village as a way to convey her new understanding to the rest of the profession.

The participants—other historians—have not arrived to be entertained. They will participate in order to assess the visual model created by the historian. They will not require any sign that reads "this is not the past" for they are well trained to know the difference between the reality of the past and the virtuality of this simulation. Once inside, the professional historians interact and participate just like any other participant, but they are equipped with different assumptions, different reasons for participating. They bring to the simulation a sensitivity to issues of causation and are prepared to assess any counterfactual outcomes the model might permit. The audience brings to the simulation an understanding of how the social space of the medieval village has been traditionally pictured by other historians; thus their participation involves an awareness of the nuances of interpretation. They also bring along an understanding of larger historiographic themes and implicitly compare this virtual display to other displays they have participated in. Thus, these participants see not only "the past" but all the other virtual reality displays that constitute the visual secondary sources of the field. The question-and-answer session following the simulation is devoted to the new insights that the simulation revealed to the participants. There are questions about the sources, disagreements with and accolades for the new interpretation, and comparisons between opposing participant outcomes.

When our procedural author returns to her home institution, she includes this "publication" on her curriculum vita as evidence of her professional activity and, she hopes, proof of her suitability for tenure. Given the technical complexity of virtual reality, it is more than likely that she is a member of a collaborative team, but a team over which she has ultimate design decision authority, like the director of a film or the architect of a building. Multiple authorship is commonly accepted in the sciences, less so in history, an institutional practice that would have to be reexamined in light of these collaborative projects. In the end, the tenure committee decides that the display counts as a publication since its chief purpose was to communicate new historical insights to other members of the profession. The virtual reality display served not only as a useful model but as a vehicle for scholarly communication.

In the above scenario, the professional conference was the site for this virtual display. There will surely be other such "sites of publication" for virtual simulations, physical locations where our hypothetical historian could display her work. Presumably conference sites would be equipped with special equipment for running virtual simulations. Large, well-endowed universities might build virtual spaces, much as they now build lecture halls, theaters, and sports stadiums. State and local governments and foundations might also build virtual reality sites in the same way they build art museums or public parks. In fact, historical museums would seem a natural site for the construction and display of virtual simulations and models. Businesses might also construct these sites in the same way they construct movie theaters. It is also possible that this virtual display could be experienced "virtually," that is, in a "shared" immersive environment by participants in widely separated physical locations. It is also possible that virtual simulations would be displayed on-line. Although these displays would not be immersive, they would allow participants to view a realistic model and to participate (that is, have the illusion of moving around) in that model. On-line publication might then include virtual reality models along with more traditional prose compositions, thereby reconfiguring our notion of a "journal."

While virtual reality displays might find a home in an electronic journal, these displays seem to tug at the traditional notion of a "publication." Unlike a traditional article or monograph, a virtual simulation appears more like an art exhibition. It would be a display of "physical" objects in a specially designed space through which large audiences would move. The display might be transitory, not permanently archived, like a museum display. The simulation might only be on display for a specified length of time, after which some smaller version of the display (comparable to a museum catalog) might survive, perhaps as an on-line nonimmersive model. While simulations might run at major conferences, procedural authors might also have their own individual "shows" to which an audience would be invited. Again, the professional legitimacy of these forms of publication depends on the rules, practices, and assumptions of the members of the discipline; they are not embedded in the technology itself.

Our hypothetical historian's well-crafted display requires more than mere attention to technical matters or stimulating graphics, or even careful primary source research. These are necessary but insufficient requirements for a useful virtual reality display. Any virtual simulation also requires attentive viewers who understand that the past can never be brought to life, that the model is not the thing modeled, and that virtual reality is more virtual than reality. "This is not the past," our sign would have to read. "It is a useful device for thinking about the past."

Chapter Five

History Takes Shape

Forbes magazine publishes a regular feature called a "charticle." As the name implies, the charticle is a large diagram, graph, or chart that plots out economic and financial trends, with accompanying text to explicate the image. The charticles are usually simple diagrams displaying one or two variables of economic data without much visual clutter. While perhaps not as information-rich as the best visualizations, the charticles do avoid much of the "chartjunk" characteristic of lesser quality publications, thus approaching the 1.0 data ink/nondata ink ratio recommended by Edward Tufte. My interest in charticles is not so much as a prototypical model for constructing visualizations, however, but rather as a publication idea. Unlike the typical diagram found in such business publications, the chart is the main article, blown up in size to cover two entire pages, and is not simply a supplementary background diversion used to illustrate or break up blocks of text. With the figure/ground relationship thus reversed, the prose explication recedes into the background, serving as the written supplement to the informational image.

I imagine that there are some disheartened critics who see the charticles appearing in a respectable magazine like *Forbes* as an example of the "dumbing down" of our society, where serious publications reduce the amount of prose contained within their pages, to be replaced by "diversionary pictures." I will not revisit this debate here, as chapter 2 was devoted to the notion that "cognitive art" is a useful way to convey meaningful information, as useful as a page of prose. Instead, I would like to explore the idea of something like a charticle as a vehicle for conveying scholarly information in history. Given the increased use of abstract visualizations in cyberspace, it is entirely possible that historians might also publish "digital charticles" in lieu of traditional prose articles.

A charticle is an example of an abstract visualization, a picture of a concept or idea. To recall, in an abstract visualization the information designer arranges symbols in a nonrepresentational abstract space. The arrangement of those symbols can be in either two or three dimensions depending upon the space. The advantage of an abstract visualization is that, unlike a page of prose, symbols stand in multidimensional syntactic relationship to each other, thus maintaining the simultaneity, structure, and holistic part-and-whole relationships that written prose linearizes.

These structural advantages are clearly present in a representational visualization, like a virtual reality simulation, but these same structural properties apply to the display of abstract ideas and concepts as well. In an abstract visualization, concepts are displayed in a nonintuitively spatial fashion; that is, the information designer provides spatial form to ideas and concepts that are not usually perceived as spatial. For example, in the charticle above, symbols indicating long-term stock market activity are arranged within a two-dimensional abstract Cartesian space, a form that exists solely in the mind of the creator of the visualization. That is, we would not find such a structure anywhere in the natural world. Abstract visualizations, then, provide shape and form to ideas and concepts. Like the writer who fashions the world in one-dimensional linear form, the creator of an abstract visualization fashions the world in two- and three-dimensional spatial form.

Despite their structural and syntactical differences and the differing shapes of the concepts and ideas, a page of prose and an abstract visualization are more analogous than we might at first realize. Both are "emblems of mind,"[1] maps of abstract terrain, visible gestures of thought. Both written prose and abstract visualizations depend upon symbol, syntax, and abstract space. Consider the page of prose you are looking at now: like a diagram or chart, a page is an abstract, nonrepresentational space upon which a writer arranges symbols (in this case, written words). These symbols refer to concepts and objects and are arranged in this abstract space according to formal rules of syntax. That syntax, as we have noted before, is one-dimensional; thus a page of prose shapes ideas and concepts in a linear fashion. In this way, prose linearizes concepts and ideas that are not inherently linear.

Like a page of prose, an abstract visualization spatializes concepts and ideas that are not inherently spatial. An abstract visualization is also a syntactical arrangement of symbols in an abstract space. Those symbols might be words but are just as likely to be lines, geometric shapes, representational images, or numbers that, nevertheless, refer to ideas and concepts. Because of the range of symbols and the multidimensional syntax, abstract visualizations shape ideas in spatial rather than linear form, allowing the information designer to escape the one-dimensionality of prose. In fact, one might be tempted to ask if ideas and concepts have any sort of inherent shape or form, or if such form is always and everywhere a product of the mind of the information designer and the representational geometry he chooses to depict such concepts.

When we approach the issue from this formalist vantage point, the charticle and a regular prose article begin to appear strangely very much alike. Both are quite different from the virtual simulations described in the previous chapter. Where a virtual reality model is a picture of a real space, both written prose and abstract visualizations are imagined spaces; where a virtual simulation is about picturing things, objects, and concrete bodies, prose and abstract visualizations are about picturing concepts and ideas. Spanish and French are very different languages, but when placed in the context of all the world's languages, their similarities become apparent. Similarly, prose and abstract visualizations are very different from each other—as we have stated throughout this book—but when placed in the context of all the world's symbolic objects, their similarities become more apparent.

As we noted previously, abstract visualizations are quickly becoming an important emblem of mind in cyberspace. Because we have long championed prose as our medium of scholarly thought and communication, it is clear that historians are comfortable with abstract emblems of mind as a way to give shape to ideas. Our profession, however, is still some distance away from accepting a "digital charticle" as a legitimate form of publication. This reluctance must be viewed as a convention, a choice professional historians make rather than any inherent weaknesses in abstract visualizations. As computers become more ubiquitous and as the ability to display complex abstract visualizations concomitantly increases, historians might very well make that cognitive leap from thinking of the past as a written line to thinking of the past as a two- or three-dimensional shape.

Pictoriacy

The actual historic impact of the computer has been as a graphics tool more than as a processor of words. With the appearance of fourth-generation computers in the 1980s, digital graphics have become commonplace in our symbolic landscape. These graphics include the virtual models described in the last chapter as well as more abstract data images, which are especially important in the sciences.

In the sciences, changes in the ability to "see" have long been an indispensable part of the enterprise.[2] Euclidean geometry provided the Western mind a visual means of ordering abstract ideas, as well as a practical tool for designing objects and structures. Leonardo Da Vinci and Albrecht Dürer were at the forefront of the scientific revolution, for both understood that sight was a critical intellectual faculty and that the ability to understand the world was a function of our ability to accurately observe it. To that end, Renaissance artists pioneered one-point perspective, which among other things allowed for the rendering of three-dimensional space on a flat surface. The development of the coordinate system, yet another indispensable tool of science, opened up new areas of mathematical exploration. Tables, schematics, and diagrams served as visual tools for the organization of statistical data. Mercator's projection—despite its distortions—served not only as a means of displaying knowledge of the earth, but also as a tool of exploration; once one could see the whole earth, one could the more easily explore it.[3] The telescope and, shortly thereafter, the microscope allowed scientists to observe worlds very large and very small. In short, extending our power to see has been an important part of the expansion of human knowledge.

It is in this context that the computer takes on historical significance, as a tool for seeing. The visual properties of computers have opened up new areas of mathematical and scientific investigation. Nowhere is this more evident than with the emergence of "nonlinear science." Chaos theory, strange attractors, dynamic equilibrium, and similar subfields were born from computer graphics, allowing scientists to see areas of information long believed to be irrelevant or simply beyond our capacity to understand.

The computer provided mathematicians and scientists a space within which to compose abstract visual models. Edward Lorenz used computers to calculate meteorological data in an effort to model long-term patterns in the weather. His research yielded the now famous "Butterfly Effect," which holds that small local changes in the weather can have much larger global effects on that system. To reach this conclusion, Lorenz used an early form of computer graphics as his chief tool of investigation. Only when he could see visual patterns in his data could the Butterfly Effect be fully understood.

Visualization was not a supplement to Lorenz's work but a central element in his thinking. He later developed a method whereby complex systems could be reduced to three equations or variables. These variables thus became the axes of an abstract space that physicists label "phase space." The state of a complex system at any moment in time could therefore be depicted as a point in this phase space. Physicists had already modeled systems that were in a steady state or whose cycles were periodic and regular; by using computer graphics, scientists like Lorenz were able to more easily depict an aperiodic system like the weather.[4] In traditional time-series graphs, such complex systems appeared hopelessly random; phase space allowed scientists the ability to see patterns in the data that were not apparent before. Phase space permits "the possibility of using a shape to help visualize the whole range of behaviors of a system," notes the science writer James Gleick. "If you can visualize the shape, you can understand the system."[5] Computers were helpful not only in crunching the numbers but in graphically organizing those numbers into a useful and meaningful form.

Scientists interested in other nonlinear phenomena created similar abstract shapes, such as Poincaré maps, bifurcation diagrams, and fractal geometries. Perhaps the most famous of these new computer-enabled shapes is the Mandelbrot set. A computer scientist at IBM, Benoit Mandelbrot became interested in the work of Gaston Julia and Pierre Fatou, who explored irregular shapes that now bear the name Julia sets. These were distorted shapes that did not conform to the rules of Euclidean geometry. Mandelbrot had access to computing power that Julia and Fatou did not; he used the computer to explore iterative equations of the type that produce Julia sets. These equations are deceptively simple, in that the iteration process masks the complexities that are inherent in such calculations. Only when Mandelbrot used the graphics capabilities of the computer did the complexity of the mathematical object that bears his name become apparent.[6] With improved graphics and the addition of color, the full implications of the Mandelbrot set could then be realized. By clicking on regions of the set, the user opens up whole new vistas of exploration, revealing new and ever emerging datascapes.

The Mandelbrot set became something of a popular icon in the late 1980s, appearing on conference brochures, books, and even poster art and t-shirts, evoking in some viewers memories of tie-dye psychedelia. The visual attractiveness and popularity of the image, however, should not detract from its real significance as an abstract visualization. Only when one could see the set could mathematical exploration then begin. The ideas of complexity, fractal geometry, and other nonlinear phenomena had long been dimly perceived by mathematicians and scientists, but before computer graphics these phenomena were always beyond reach. In this way, observes Douglas Hofstadter, "the digital computer plays the role of Magellan's ship, the astronomer's telescope, and the physicist's accelerator." Just as these other tools of scientific exploration had to become larger and faster in order to aid our understanding, "so one would need computers of ever greater size, speed and accuracy in order to explore the remoter regions of mathematical space."[7]

These computer graphics, it should be clear by now, are not simply pretty pictures and diversions from the "real work." "This way of doing mathematics," concludes Hofstadter, "builds powerful visual imagery and *intuitions* directly into one's understanding"[8] of the math and science. Images here are not simply illustrations, but are the central cognitive objects of the disciplinary exercise. Thus, when Hofstadter claims that computer graphics build visual intuition into mathematical understanding, he means that visual thinking moves to the core of the enterprise.

"Scientific visualization" has not remained confined to just science, however. Abstract data images are quickly becoming part of other disciplines, as will be explored below. This is what computer scientists mean when they observe that more and more information in cyberspace is being shaped into spatial form. The implication, then, is that the visual intuition identified by Hofstadter is seeping into other areas outside of the sciences. "To develop an intuition for this kind of knowledge," notes the historian Alan Beyerchen, "all of us, not just research mathematicians and scientists, will have to sharpen a new (but also . . . very ancient) skill to augment those of literacy and numeracy." Beyerchen refers to this skill as "pictoriacy," by which he means "the capacity to deal effectively with complex images and the data they embody."[9] The geographer Mark Monmonier refers to this same skill as "graphicacy," meaning "fluency with graphs, maps, diagrams, and photographs." Monmonier would include graphicacy along with literacy, articulacy, and numeracy as the core communication skills of, in his words, "the educated person [and] the complete scholar."[10] Note that both of these definitions identify abstract images as meaningful vehicles of thought and expression.

Beyerchen makes reference to the notion that "pictoriacy" is an "ancient skill." Indeed, the ability to picture abstract ideas appears to be as old as linguistic and mathematical skills—perhaps even older—and is not only a function of the computer revolution. In fact, abstract images might be defined as our first form of information. The historians Michael Hobart and Zachary Schiffman define "information" as "mental objects separated from the flux of experience."[11] Humans took an important evolutionary step when they began to store ideas in material form, what the psychologist Merlin Donald refers to as "external symbolic storage."[12] Once frozen in form, those mental objects could be stored, recalled, exchanged, and analyzed. In contrast, gesture and speech—our first forms of communication—do not count as information in Hobart and Schiffman's scheme, since neither are abstracted from direct experience, nor are they preserved in material form. In fact, "evanescent speech is part of that very flow, communicating information without necessarily creating or preserving it."[13] To Hobart and Schiffman, written alphabets were humanity's first forms of information. Writing, in their estimation, "gives stability to the mental objects abstracted from the flow of experience, such that one can access them readily and repeatedly."[14]

If we accept Hobart and Schiffman's very useful definition, we could easily argue that the birth of information lies with the creation of the first images, long before the invention of writing. Consider the small human figurine art historians have dubbed the Venus of Willendorf. This small stone carving and many others like it were created several thousand years before the first writing systems. Given the definition above, this mental object is a type of visual information, a material form of an idea abstracted from the flow of experience. Noting her bodily exaggerations, some scholars have interpreted the Venus figure not as a physical representation of a human but as an abstraction for "life." Like the written word "life," the image for "life" is an abstraction meant to encapsulate a concept. The Venus figure, then, is not a representative image but instead a picture of an idea, a rudimentary type of abstract visualization.

Other examples abound. The cave paintings at Lascaux similarly preserved in material form moments in the flux of experience, preserving the memory of a hunt. Again, some scholars contend that rather than being a representative image of an actual hunt, the paintings served a more metaphorical and abstract function as a totem ensuring "life" and "bounty." The archaeologist and anthropologist Elizabeth Wayland Barber contends that early humans developed textiles and clothing not so much for warmth and protection—not really necessary on the savanna—but as a type of communication system. "Clothing," she contends, "has been the handiest solution to conveying social messages visually, silently [and] continuously." (We see contemporary evidence of this when we see a bride wearing a white gown; the message is "I am getting married.") Cloth, whether in the form of clothing, tapestries, or wall hangings, has long served as a bearer of meaning, sometimes conveying social rank and status, sometimes serving as a memory keeper. "Patterned cloth," Barber contends, "is infinitely variable and, like language, can encode arbitrarily any message whatever."[15] Visual patterns on cloth encoded abstract information, making these mental objects candidates for early forms of "information." My point here is not to play the game of proving which type of information came first, but rather to suggest that "pictoriacy" is as ancient and fundamental as literacy.

That skill seems to be hardwired into every human, not only in those perceived to have artistic skill. The ability to encode abstract ideas like "life" and "marriage" into visual form is a fundamental part of every human's cognitive toolbox. Rudolf Arnheim described an experiment conducted by his students in which subjects were asked to draw nonmimetic images of abstract concepts like "democracy" and "the future."[16] (Anyone who has played the party game Pictionary will immediately recognize this exercise, one of the more popular assignments in my Visual Thinking class.) The subjects were not to use representative images or mimetic symbols—that is, those visual signs referring to concrete objects—but only lines, dots, shapes, and textures. None of the subjects was "artistically gifted," yet the results were striking, as the subjects produced subtle abstract images to represent the concepts. Subjects drew "democracy," for instance, as a circle with radiating lines or as an oval containing various lines and shapes, suggesting inclusion and unity. Arnheim's point was to demonstrate that this exercise pulled unconscious thoughts to the level of consciousness in a way words and language cannot; however, I believe a more significant implication is the demonstration that abstract visual thinking of this type is a fundamental skill common to all.

The art educator Betty Edwards used this exercise in her own teaching to prove that everyone has the ability to draw. Influenced by Arnheim, she also saw these "analog drawings" as a window into a deeper unconscious. By analog, Edwards means "making subjective thought objective by giving it visible form."[17] Like Arnheim, Edwards asked students to create nonmimetic drawings of abstract ideas; she took the further step of grouping together the student drawings and comparing the finished results. Edwards perceived common visual patterns in several of the drawings. Images depicting "femininity," for example, featured criss-crossing lines; images for "depression" were dark and seemed to fill the lower half of the page, since depression connotes "low" or "down." These students worked independently and were not looking at each other's work. Edwards thus saw this convergence of common visual forms of nonmimetic representation as evidence for some sort of Chomskian visual "deep structure," paralleling a type of Jungian collective unconscious.

While the idea that these drawings tap into a visual archetype might be a bit overstated, the experiments of Arnheim and Edwards suggest at the very least that all people can draw upon a form of "pictoriacy" that allows them to think about abstract concepts in visual form. Analog drawings demonstrate that, like linguistic ability, all humans have the ability to think in terms of abstract visualizations. Like the carver of the Venus of Willendorf, the participants in these experiments created visual mental objects that were, in Arnheim's words, "purely cognitive, not different in principle from what scientists show in their schematic designs."[18]

The Mandelbrot set, nonmimetic analog drawings, and patterned cloth all seem to derive from the same cognitive source. Each gives visible shape and form to abstract, nonmimetic ideas. Therefore, the appearance of larger numbers of abstract visualizations in cyberspace should not be viewed as evidence of "dumbing down," but of a resurgence of an ancient, expressive form of thought and communication.

Conceptual Cartography

The abstract visualizations enabled by computers are not as revolutionary as they might seem, but are part of a long line of visual mental objects dating back millennia. As noted before, many of these visual forms can be found in disciplines outside of the sciences and mathematics. Historians may well find useful examples here. In each of these cases below, the function of the abstract image is not to entertain or to serve as an illustration but to act as the main carrier of the information. In each case, the visualization is dense with data, not decoration.

In the practice of history, maps have been the most widely accepted form of visualization. As we noted in chapter 3, historians will readily accord a map the status of "serious" history, keeping in mind that the map is used as a supplement to a written account. While historians might be some distance from adopting digitized abstract visualizations into their professional work, maps might serve as a useful entry into that symbolic realm. A map, recall, is a representational space—some portion of the surface of the earth—wherein one arranges meaningful symbols. When making a map we want to highlight certain features of the terrain and the activities that occur on that terrain and represent those features using visual symbols. In his Web-based article on revolutionary France, Robert Darnton includes an interactive map of Paris.[19] By clicking on numbers representing sections of the city, one can descend into various wards, then click on the text of police reports. This display suggests interesting ways to imagine abstract visualizations for historical inquiries. Although he wrote an accompanying prose narrative, Darnton's map might be treated and used as the main interface with the data. Rather than organizing the narrative in the form of a linear prose word-model, the map could function as the narrative, organizing the data in multidimensional visual and spatial form. Darnton's map is a very rudimentary type of geographic information system.

Geographic information systems (GIS) represent a prominent form of mapmaking in the electronic environment that historians might find useful as a tool for visualization. The U.S. Geological Survey defines GIS as "a computer system capable of assembling, storing, manipulating and displaying geographically referenced information, i.e. data identified according to their locations [in geographic space]."[20] On the surface, GIS maps would appear to be simply a digital version of an ancient symbolic form, yet there are important differences between a GIS map and a traditional map.

The first difference relates to the construction of the map. A GIS display takes data from a variety of databases and converts them into visual form. For example, a traditional topographic map, satellite imagery, census data, and rainfall amounts can all be entered into the system. These are then converted into a uniform spatial form, meaning that all the data are standardized in terms of the same geographic space. Note that the original data, such as the tabular census data or the information on rainfall, need not be in spatial form initially. As long as that data can be expressed within an x, y, z coordinate system measuring longitude, latitude, and elevation, it can be "translated" into a GIS display.[21] The only requirement is that the data need to have the potential to be converted into spatial form.

The second difference between GIS and a traditional map concerns the layering and analysis of information (Figure 5.1). Once these various data sets have been entered into the system, a researcher can discern patterns and relationships between those data. Recall the map transparency exercise I described in chapter 3, where I placed a map of the spread of Christianity on top of a map of the trade routes of the Roman Empire. The purpose of that exercise was to discern how the empire enabled the spread of the religion, revealing that Christianity was initially confined to urban areas and well-traveled shipping and overland routes. That simple exercise is similar to what GIS enables. All those data sets can be layered on top of each other in order to discern relationships between the data. Thus, GIS serves as a tool of both inquiry and analysis. The researcher can inquire into those data by asking questions: what is the relationship between traffic patterns and urban growth patterns? where would be a good place to locate this factory? Additionally, in some cases, GIS can be used as a simulation tool, to forecast future "what if?" scenarios. A researcher could ask, for example, what the effect of a gasoline spill in this particular area would be. This layering function and the inquiry into and analysis of data that it enables makes a GIS display a type of interactive map.[22]

A third difference between GIS and a traditional map concerns the function of the resulting display. Both types of maps involve communicating visual information to a wide audience. Rather than serving as a supplement to some written narrative, however, the GIS display is the chief narrative, the main interface with the data. Visualization here serves not as an attention-grabbing trick, but rather as the main vehicle for thinking about and expressing patterns and relationships in the data. Like a prose composition, the GIS display is both the user's interface with the data and the template that orders one's thinking about those data.

The applications of GIS to the study of history should seem apparent. An historian of early modern Spain and of world systems history, J.B. Owens has explored some of these applications. For Owens, world history involves the study of "regular, interaction networks of varying density linking loci over an often global space."[23] He found his understanding of world history clouded by the teleological, linearizing assumptions enabled by written prose. Owens uses GIS as a way to picture complex, multidimensional networks of interaction, although the technique can be applied to other areas of research, not just world history.

Owens describes a research project using GIS. The display "involves organizing data in terms of system-oriented concepts like points, lines, and polygons forming complex geometric shapes, each of which will express a type of patterned interaction during a particular period." All historians can

Figure 5.1 **GIS As Layers of Maps**. By layering information in cartographic form, a user can discern visual patterns between the various levels of data. A complex GIS display is as intricate as a written article; historians might one day accept such a display in lieu of a dissertation, journal article, or conference presentation.

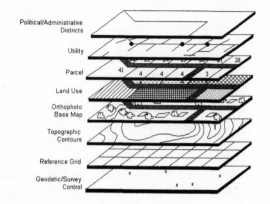

Source: Urban and Regional Information Systems Association. Reprinted with permission.

be said to study "patterned interaction during a particular period," only rather than points, lines, and polygons we tend to favor words, sentences, and prose. "Available information must be converted into geo-referenced spatial databases corresponding to a common geographic reference system," meaning that the information must be converted into spatial form and depicted within a representational geographic space.

> Data about particular locations, its human population for example, can be expressed in reference to points or polygons. Data about interactions between two locations can be expressed as lines. Gradations in prevailing vegetation, average precipitation, language use, or religious adherence can be expressed through changes in color or design. Each of these matters can be treated as a thematic layer that can be linked to the others and to the geographic reality of the region . . . each type of information will appear as an overlay containing complex geometric shapes. It will then be possible to observe changes in these shapes over time, and by stacking them on top of each other, to explore interactions among them.[24]

In this way, the GIS display allows the presentation of several variables of primary source information, meaning that the display is dense with data, not decoration. Further, the display serves as an analytic tool; the historian can inquire into those data, asking questions about location, trends, and patterns. In so interacting with the map, the historian can explore simultaneous, multidimensional layers of information.

Conceivably, one might also use the GIS system to explore alternative scenarios, a geographically referenced counterfactual. In the same way researchers can ask questions about future scenarios using a GIS display, an historian could ask counterfactual questions about the past using the same technology. If a variable were altered, how might the configuration of the system be changed? As we argued in the last chapter, such a thought exercise would not be a party game but a serious effort to understand causation in the past. However historians might employ it, a GIS map is not simply a supplemental display used to illustrate a written article. It is both a tool of historical inquiry and the final model by which the historian communicates his findings to a scholarly audience, a data-rich visual secondary source.

The word "map" is a convenient shorthand for "the spatialization of data." What if we were not bound to the surface of the earth, and carried out the same type of symbolic composition and analysis used in a GIS space in an abstract space? "Data mining" (sometimes called "knowledge exploration") reflects a similar type of analysis as GIS mapping. Businesses and marketers use data mining software as a way to find patterns in data from a variety of databases. Like a GIS display, the resulting data mining display reflects a visual interface with the layers of databases. Rather than displaying the results of such an inquiry in a geographically referenced space, however, the results of data mining can be displayed within an abstract three-dimensional space. For example, Figure 5.2 from IBM shows the results of a database query into credit card applications. The image depicts the abstract "location" of approved cardholders within a three-dimensional space, with the axes represented as net worth, work duration, and debt ratio. The spheres are different cardholders, the size and color of each referring to income level and credit card limits. Note that the use of dimension, shape, and color are not for decorative effect but a way to display several variables of data. Data mining is a relatively recent term describing a fairly old practice, namely statistical analysis. I have little doubt that quantitative historians or historians who regularly analyze the data in databases will be immediately attracted to this technique of discerning pattern in the noise of the data. Like a GIS display, the abstract three-dimensional display is the interface, the narrative; a prose explication would serve as a supplement to this well-formed visualization.

Data mining maps numbers and quantities. Similarly, a concept map maps ideas in a nongeographically referenced abstract space. A concept map is a general name for a class of diagrams that depict multidimensional relationships between concepts. A pioneer in the use of concept maps, Joseph Novak defines this visualization as "a tool for representing some of the concept-propositional or meaning frameworks a person has for a given concept or set of concepts."[25] Enthusiasts tout the benefits of concept mapping

Figure 5.2 **Data Mining in Three Dimensions**. Data mining is similar to GIS, in that various databases of information are "translated" into visual form in order to see patterns in the data, patterns that would not necessarily be evident were one to examine the numbers alone. Imagine exploring these data as a virtual reality display.

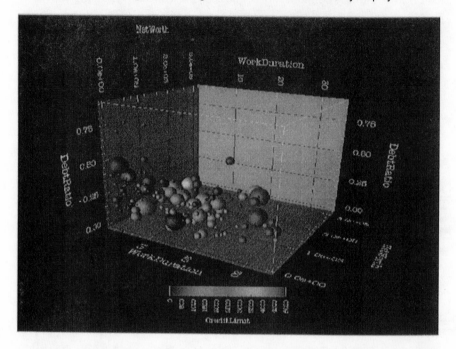

Source: Image created by Frank Suits and Peter Kirchner at the IBM T.J. Watson Research Center using the Data Explorer visualization environment, www.research. ibm.com/dx. Reprinted with permission.

for note-taking, as a group brainstorming tool and planning aid, and as a source of interesting graphics for presentations. Some theorists contend that concept maps more closely resemble the patterns of thought of the mind and are more "natural" than writing.[26] To my way of thinking, concept maps are a basic form of abstract visualization.

Most advocates define concept maps as facilitation tools, a means to enable some other end. I believe, however, that concepts maps have great potential as forms of abstract visualizations that can stand alone as the final expression of thought. These visualizations are hybrid symbolic objects, with some features of a map and some features of a page of written prose. Like prose, concept maps are built from symbols, syntax, and abstract space; like a traditional map, concepts are arranged "spatially" upon a two-dimensional abstract terrain. This hybrid nature suggests that if historians are to incorporate digital abstract visualization into their work, they might find concept maps easy and familiar symbolic objects with which to work.

Concept maps begin with "nodes."[27] In most concept maps, nodes are words or short phrases that connote a concept, which Novak defines as "a perceived regularity in events or objects, or records of events or objects, designated by a label."[28] Interestingly, Novak still designates concepts by words, as opposed to some other type of visual mark or symbol, suggesting that a concept map is, at its heart, a new way to arrange words on a page. Nodes are sometimes enclosed in a shape, although in most formal concept maps the shapes themselves convey little or no additional information.

In a concept map, nodes are linked together by lines or "arcs." These lines visually depict the relationships between two or more concepts. Lines are sometimes accompanied by connecting words that show the relationships and connections between concepts. When "two or more words [or nodes are] combined to form a statement about an event, object or idea," a "proposition" has been formed.[29] Depending upon the soundness of the connection, a proposition may be defined as "valid" or "invalid." As concepts are linked to other concepts, the meaning of those concepts grows, much in the way Douglas Hofstadter identified the "halo of meaning around words." Thus, a concept might be linked to more than one other concept, creating a web of propositions.

Like a traditional map, GIS display, or data mining visualization, concept maps link concepts together into propositions via a multidimensional syntax, yielding interesting shapes in an abstract space. Since nodes can be linked to more than one other concept, concept maps escape the one-dimensionality of written prose and enter a two-dimensional maplike abstract space. This multidimensional syntax enables a variety of shapes for concept maps:

- Flow chart map (Figure 5.3). The simplest and most basic of these shapes is a line. A flow chart map arranges concepts in a linear fashion and is in effect a type of sentence.
- Hierarchical maps (Figure 5.4). These are concept maps—which Novak himself favors—that place general concepts at the top of the abstract space. As we view down, concepts become more specific and are therefore grouped under the more general concepts.
- Systems map (Figure 5.5). In this type of concept map, concepts are arranged as a process or cycle, with inputs and outputs in the system.
- Spider map (Figure 5.6). This map places a concept at the center of the space. Propositions—that is, connections to other concepts—radiate outward from this main concept. In complex spider maps, two or more concepts serve as central hubs from which propositions radiate.

Figure 5.3 **Flow Chart Concept Maps**. Concept maps are composed from nodes and arcs, concepts and lines. The syntax of concept maps varies widely; the designer can choose from any number of arrangements of the nodes and arcs. That arrangement should not be a haphazard choice, however, for this visual syntax itself carries meaningful information. This diagram and the ones that follow depict the formal structures of this visual syntax. As this example demonstrates, a flow chart is reminiscent of a sentence, in that concepts line up.

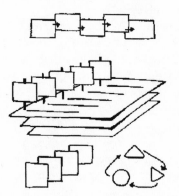

Source: Mary E. Conners, M.A. AIM Lab, College of Agricultural, Consumer and Environmental Sciences, University of Illinois at Urbana-Champaign. Reprinted with permission.

- Landscape map (Figure 5.7). Here, physical terrain and representative symbols stand for concepts. Landscape, then, is a metaphorical space upon which concepts are arranged.
- Three-demensional map (Figure 5.8). As the name implies, in this type of concept map concepts find more complex syntactic connections, since the abstract space has been expanded.
- Mandala map (Figure 5.9). This type of concept map arranges concepts in an abstract geometric pattern, often in a circle.

In each case, the rules governing the construction of the space determine the final shape of the concept map. Thus, a concept map is proselike in that it relies on symbols and syntax. It is maplike in that the syntax and the space are multidimensional:

Novak and other proponents of concept maps often describe the connections between nodes as "logical." In fact, much of the language used to describe concept maps derives from linguistics and logic. For example, note the descriptions in the above paragraphs: "concepts" are linked into

Figure 5.4 **Hierarchical Concept Maps**. In a hierarchical concept map, the more significant information is placed at the top. The diagrams of Hammurabi's society (Figure 3.3) and Chinese society (Figure 3.4) are both types of hierarchical concept maps.

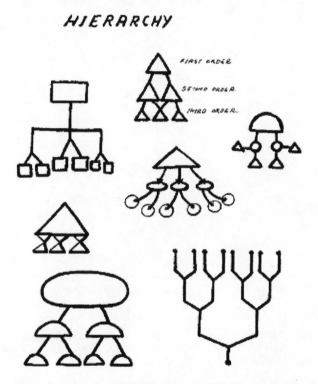

Source: Mary E. Conners, M.A. AIM Lab, College of Agricultural, Consumer and Environmental Sciences, University of Illinois at Urbana-Champaign. Reprinted with permission.

"propositions" that can be "valid" or "invalid." Nodes are "words" that are connected together by "lines," which is similar to how words are linked in written sentences. However, in a concept map these connecting lines meander in two dimensions, not just one as with written prose. Instead of having to line up words in sequential order, a concept map allows one to arrange words in two-dimensional space. One could claim, therefore, that concept maps are a type of two-dimensional visual "logic."

While this might be an adequate description, I am not convinced that "logical" is the most appropriate word to describe these types of symbolic objects. The word "logic" derives from "logos," which refers to words and language. Logic thus derives from language, which is itself linear and one-dimensional. When defining logic, we implicitly mean a

Figure 5.5 **Systems Concept Maps**.

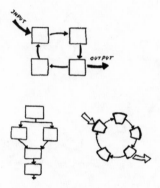

Source: Mary E. Conners, M.A. AIM Lab, College of Agricultural, Consumer and Environmental Sciences, University of Illinois at Urbana-Champaign. Reprinted with permission.

Figure 5.6 **Spider Concept Maps**. In complex spider maps, two or more concepts serve as central "hubs" from which propositions radiate. The diagram of Japan in Figure I.1 is structured as a spider concept map.

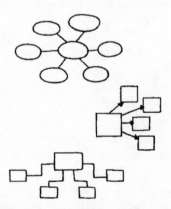

Source: Mary E. Conners, M.A. AIM Lab, College of Agricultural, Consumer and Environmental Sciences, University of Illinois at Urbana-Champaign. Reprinted with permission.

Figure 5.7 **Landscape Concept Maps**.

Source: Mary E. Conners, M.A. AIM Lab, College of Agricultural, Consumer and Environmental Sciences, University of Illinois at Urbana-Champaign. Reprinted with permission.

Figure 5.8 **Three-Dimensional Concept Maps**. All of the above concept maps arrange concepts in two dimensions. Adding a third dimensions adds the potential for more connections radiating from concepts. When we write, concepts line up in one-dimensional sequential order; in a three-dimensional concept map, concepts may be connected in a variety of ways. For other examples of three-dimensional concept maps, see Figures 5.10 and 5.11.

Source: Mary E. Conners, M.A. AIM Lab, College of Agricultural, Consumer and Environmental Sciences, University of Illinois at Urbana-Champaign. Reprinted with permission.

Figure 5.9 **Mandala Concept Maps**. Mandalas are abstract, intricate geometric patterns usually associated with religious symbolism, often depicting circles, wholeness, and unity. The sketch in Figure 2.2 is organized as a type of mandala.

▲ MANDALA

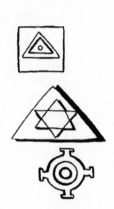

Source: Mary E. Conners, M.A. AIM Lab, College of Agricultural, Consumer and Environmental Sciences, University of Illinois at Urbana-Champaign. Reprinted with permission.

one-dimensional form of thought. Since logic is the formalization of language and since language is one-dimensional, the formalization of language must also be one-dimensional. Thus "logic," if we are to keep the original connotation, cannot exist in more than one dimension.

If we wish to expand the connotations of that word to include two- and three-dimensional syntactical relationships between words and concepts, then "logic" is still a valid word. However, we might also wish to retain the conceptual relationship between "logic" and "language" and instead use another word for the valid multidimensional connections in a concept map or any other abstract data map. Candidates include words like "analogical," "associative," and "relational."[30] Unfortunately, these words do not connote the same notions of rigor and validity in the same way as "logic" does. We might wish, then, to coin a new word to describe a visualization that depicts well-formed, valid, simultaneous, and multidimensional relationships between concepts. "Eikonical" might serve well. If "logic" derives from the Greek word for "word," "eikonic" derives from the Greek word for "image." Thus, when I say that concept maps are not "logical," I am not suggesting that they are not well-formed or rigorous. Quite the contrary: a well-formed concept map is eikonical.

Whether one labels these well-formed images logical, relational, or eikonical, concept maps could serve historians well not just as a facilitation tool but as a medium of thought and expression. For example, instead of using these visualizations as simply a note-taking or brainstorming device, historians might submit a elaborate concept map to a journal in lieu of a written essay. Peer reviewers would look for scholarly rigor, primary source research, and the validity of the propositions. Software has been developed that makes creating concept maps fairly easy, although one could just as readily make them by hand. There would be many applications in the training of apprentice historians. Following Novak's lead, teachers could give students a short list of perhaps a half a dozen words (concepts) that they must link together into meaningful multidimensional propositions.[31] The form of the concept map would be the student's choice. In evaluating the final product, the teacher would assess the validity of the arcs between concepts and whether the map is dense with data or just decoration. Novak has students submit an equally weighted oral or written report, but if it is well-formed, there is no reason why a concept map could not stand alone as a student's formal expression of her understanding.

Concept maps are one cognitive avenue through which students can express their understanding of important historical concepts. These student exercises might also "scale up" to serve as evocative forms of scholarly thought and communication. Alaric Dickinson uses "cause boxes" as an evaluative tool to gauge the understanding of the students, even those with poor written compositional skills.[32] Cause boxes are essentially a type of concept map (Figure 5.10). Students are asked some historical question, such as "Why did the Romans conquer Britain?" They are given six boxes, each with a picture and a short phrase representing a concept, such as "The Roman Empire was rich" and "The Romans had well-trained, well-equipped soldiers." Students must then draw lines connecting these cause boxes into such a configuration that they explain the final result. They may use one, some, or all of the boxes in picturing the connections between causes, and lines may connect two or more boxes simultaneously. All lines must ultimately lead to the final result, which is depicted as a box in the center of the diagram with the instruction "explain this box" printed below. The result is a multivariate image that depicts simultaneous, multidimensional causation rather than a linear chain of causes.

This exercise could be applied to a host of historical questions. Imagine a student answering the question "Why did Europe go to war in 1914?" by drawing a concept map intricately linking "imperialism," "jingoism," "the Balkans," and other nodes of causes together into a mandala or systems map. In so choosing the resulting shape, the student would be making decisions as to the relative weight of the causes, their place in the larger narrative, the

Figure 5.10   **Cause Boxes**.

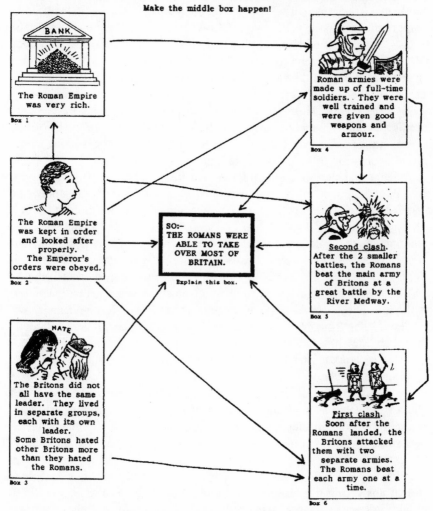

Question 12. Why were the Romans able to take over?

[The boxes on this Chart are not in any special order]
Choose any boxes which help explain why the Romans were able to take over.
Join them up with arrows to show best why the Romans were able to take over.
Make the best explanation you can.
An arrow from one box to another means: the first box helps explain the second box.
Use as many joins as you need. You can have more than one arrow to or from a box.
BUT don't make joins that don't help explain why the Romans were able to take over.

Make the middle box happen!

The Roman Empire
was very rich.
Box 1

Roman armies were
made up of full-time
soldiers. They were
well trained and
were given good
weapons and
armour.
Box 4

The Roman Empire
was kept in order
and looked after
properly.
The Emperor's
orders were obeyed.
Box 2

SO:-
THE ROMANS WERE
ABLE TO TAKE
OVER MOST OF
BRITAIN.

Explain this box.

Second clash.
After the 2 smaller
battles, the Romans
beat the main army
of Britons at a
great battle by the
River Medway.
Box 5

The Britons did not
all have the same
leader. They lived
in separate groups,
each with its own
leader.
Some Britons hated
other Britons more
than they hated
the Romans.
Box 3

First clash.
Soon after the
Romans landed, the
Britons attacked
them with two
separate armies.
The Romans beat
each army one at a
time.
Box 6

Source: Alaric Dickinson, "Progression in Children's Thinking and Understanding in History," in Allan Martin, Lez Smart, and David Yeomans, eds. *Information Technology and the Teaching of History: International Perspectives.* (Amsterdam: Harwood Academic Publishers, 1977), 114. Reprinted with permission.

difference between long-term and proximate causes, and the degree of simultaneity between causes. To make the task even more challenging, students might be asked to devise their own cause boxes and then to construct the propositional links between them. When evaluating such pictures of ideas, the teacher's task is to assess the validity of the propositional connections and the density of the data.

Depending upon each student's particular understanding of causation, the concept maps take on different configurations. Dickinson has identified at least three classes. In a "narrativizing response," the student links the boxes in a linear order: first this happened, which leads to this cause, which leads to this, which yields the result in the middle. This response is proselike, viewing causation as a sentence and suggesting that a concept map may not be the most appropriate form of expression in this case. In an "additive response," the value of the map becomes apparent. In this case, the student shows several causes all converging at one point, like an inverse spider map, with causes radiating inward. This is a visual depiction of simultaneous causation, which is very difficult to describe in written form. In an "analytic response," the boxes are linked together in complex ways, some boxes linked to two or more other boxes. As Dickinson explains, "Background conditions are picked out as separate starting points for different, sometimes separate and sometimes interlinked, causal chains which lead into the events for which they are conditions."[33] Thus, cause boxes are not simply dumbed-down substitutes for unlettered students, but a useful way of picturing simultaneous and complex types of causation, something like an abstract version of the diagrams in William McNeill's *The Rise of the West* that we encountered in chapter 3. Whichever form of response they choose, Dickinson's students exhibit sophisticated understanding of history through these shapes of causation, shapes historians might find useful as a way to picture the multidimensionality of causation.

A cause box concept map of some interesting historical question could also serve the professional historian well as a useful organizational interface with digitized information. In fact, some Web site designers are suggesting that concept maps could be used as an effective interface in cyberspace.[34] Presented with a concept map, a user could click on a node as a way to fetch the information. Douglas Cremer uses something like a concept map as an interface to organize his world history survey. He has created "The Cube of World History," which he defines as "a virtual three-dimensional space containing text, image, print sources, and web links to a wide variety of topics in world history" (Figure 5.11). In this 5×5×5 cube, geography, chronology, and category serve as the three dimensions. The resulting space is then "filled up" by arranging information within the

Figure 5.11 **Cube of World History**. Rather than a line—this, then this, then this—the cube organizes historical information as a three-dimensional space. As with other visualizations, one could view the whole, then zoom into the parts. History seems less teleological—moving inexorably in a line toward one point—when imagined as a cube.

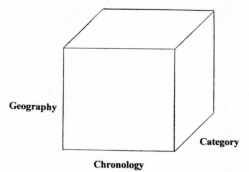

Source: Douglas J. Cremer, "The Cube of World History," www.woodbury.edu/ faculty/dcremer/the_cube/cubiclg.htm. Reprinted with permission.

resulting 125 points inside the cube. Thus, if I wanted to locate information on African art in the fifteenth century, I would click the appropriate node.[35] While Cremer does not mention it, those 125 nodes could also be linked together with arcs to create visible propositions, allowing a user to see connections within the entire space at the same time she can descend into specific data, thus maintaining whole/part relationships. In an analogous manner as a textbook, the cube serves as a three-dimensional clickable concept map for organizing historical narrative.

That narrative is given shape by the cube. In the same way that a prose account shapes historical information into a line, the cube shapes that information in a three-dimensional space. Furthermore, by altering the shape of the narrative, we could, presumably, alter our understanding of the larger historical metanarrative. What if our three-dimensional shape were a pyramid rather than a cube? The information in that concept map would appear to be ascending toward a final apex, something like a visual "end of history" scenario reminiscent of Hegel or Marx or Fukuyama. If the pyramid were inverted, the nodes would appear to explode from some original ur-point, something like an historical big bang. What if our shape were a cylinder? How would the arcs between nodes then be constrained, and how would this affect our understanding of the movement of history through time and space? What if the shape were a sphere? The exterior of that sphere could be the surface of the earth; as one clicked into the interior of the sphere, one could move back through time, in the way Fernand Braudel organized his *History of Civilizations.* Computer scientists use three-dimensional "hyperbolic

Figure 5.12 **Three-Dimensional Hyperbolic Space.** What if the cube of world history (Figure 5.10) were instead organized as a three-dimensional sphere? How would this choice affect the metanarrative of history?

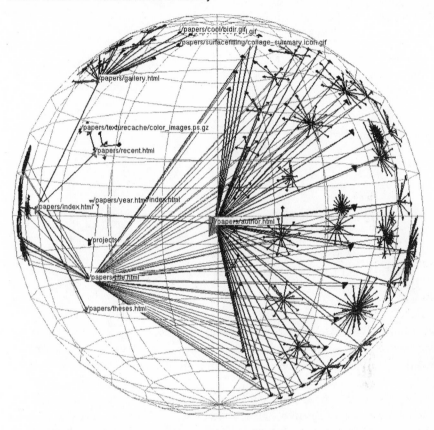

Source: Tamara Munzner, "H3: Laying Out Directed Graphics in 3-D Hyperbolic Space," *Proceedings of the 1997 Symposium on Information Visualization,* October 20–21, 1997, Phoenix, Arizona, pp. 2–10. © 1997 IEEE. Reprinted with permission.

spaces" to represent complex structures like the World Wide Web (Figure 5.12). Historians might well use similar spaces to map out the complexities of world history.

A Braudelian hyperbolic space, a cylinder, a pyramid, and a cube would each reflect a different metanarrative for how the historian has decided to shape the past. This would not be a particularly new development in historical scholarship. Speculative philosophers of history have long sought to expose the underlying geometric shape of the past, whether that be a line, a circle, a spiral, or a cycle. These historians have long thought in one-dimensional

Figure 5.13 **Network Visualization of !Kung Gift Exchange**. In this image from Germany, "spheres and lines arranged in space" elegantly depict four variables of data (flow, amount, origin, and distance) with almost no "chartjunk."

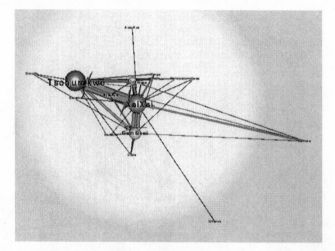

Source: Lothar Krempel, "Hxaro Gift Exchange among the !Kung San in Botswana and Namibia," www.mpi-fg-koeln.mpg.de/~lk/netvis/kungsregion.html. Reprinted with permission.

shapes, as opposed to the two- and three-dimensional shapes suggested above. Rather than serving merely as a written metaphor, however, these shapes would provide visible, concrete representation and organization of our ideas of historical metanarrative.

Concept maps, then, could serve as a useful means of organizing historical information. They might also serve as useful cognitive objects in their own right, even as the final product of historical research, at once an organizational template and the interface with a professional audience. The types of concept maps professional historians might use would need to be a great deal more sophisticated than schoolchildren's cause boxes, but the basic principles would be the same. For example, concepts might be designated by representative images or abstract symbols, not just words. The relative size and shape of the nodes might also denote differences between concepts. Propositional lines would not be confined to one size, but could have different thickness, thus identifying differences in the strength of the bonds between concepts. The distance between nodes might suggest the distance and proximity between concepts. Concept maps might also be layered on top of each other, as in a GIS display, revealing patterns and relationships between maps. All of these techniques would not be used for decorative purposes but as a way to convey more variables of data in the same constricted space. When the basic elements of

Figure 5.14 **Network Visualization of a Petition Movement During the Revolution of 1848.** This is one frame of an animated diagram. The small circles represent individuals and are arranged in clusters according to their participation in a series of events depicted as grey spheres. Shading is used in this image to indicate the degree to which these individuals were exposed to revolutionary activities. Changes in shading, then, show changes in the level of exposure. Since the visualization is animated, the shape changes configuration and shading as changes in the movement occur. "Change through time" is thus depicted as "change in shape."

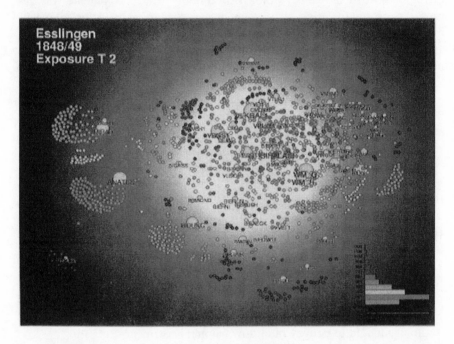

Source: Lothar Krempel, "The Growth of a Petition Movement in a Structure of City Linked Events," www.mpi-fg-koeln.mpg.de/~lk/netvis/mobil/mobil.html. Reprinted with permission.

this conceptual cartography are thus extended, historians could then create elaborate data-rich abstract visualizations.

These data-rich visualizations would be more complex than a simple bar graph or pie chart of numbers. Take, for instance, the "network visualizations" developed at the Max Planck Institute. One visualization depicts the patterns of gift exchange among the !Kung in Botswana and Namibia (Figure 5.13). The spheres represent the regions from which gifts arrive, and the lines show the patterns of distribution, reminiscent of nodes and arcs in a concept map. The visualization also shows the relative geographic distances of these regions. Thus, this abstract visualization elegantly depicts four variables of data (flow, amount, origin, distance) with almost no "chartjunk."

In another network visualization, researchers have depicted the evolving shape of a petition movement during the Revolutions of 1848 in Germany (Figure 5.14). The image shows "1200 individuals as small spheres. Each individual is placed according to his pattern of participation in one or more of over 60 events. The events are shown as gray spheres, their size stands for the number of participants." Color is used in this image to indicate "the degree of exposure to activists"; thus changes in color convey historical meaning and are not simply an attention-grabbing trick. Further, this image is animated, meaning that the shape changes configuration and color as changes in the movement occur. "Change through time" is thus depicted as "change in shape." This visualization was created from a database of historical documents, demonstrating that the visualization serves not only as an elegant display but as a useful organizer of historical information. Like prose, the abstract visualization is a template for ideas.

In another interesting visualization, researchers created a shape depicting "the structure of world trade" (Figure 5.15). The visualization displays several variables of data simultaneously. The size of the spheres for each country shows volume flows; the thickness of the links stands for the volume of trade between countries; color distinguishes regional blocs. This image reflects data from 1981 to 1992; like the previous image, it seems amenable to animation. Watching the structure change shape would not be simply an amusement designed to hook viewers in but would serve as another meaningful dimension of information. More dense with data than a typical diagram or chart, and reminiscent of the complex visualizations of Minard and Horrabin, all of these visualizations reflect the advantages of using a spatial idiom of thought to convey multidimensional networks of relations.

Given their weblike complexity, it would also be interesting to experience a virtual reality version of these network visualizations. In the last chapter, I briefly noted that some researchers have begun to wed abstract computer images to virtual reality technology. The effect is to take an abstract image like the network visualizations, turn them into three-dimensional "dataspaces," and invite viewers to "fly around and climb inside" these structures of data. In the above case, viewers could observe the topography of the "shape of world trade" from whichever perspective they wished and could fly into the complex center of this interesting cognitive object. Such a display would allow viewers the opportunity to "empathize" and "interact" with abstract data in the same way they would with physical objects and physical space. Our understanding of abstract data would now include direct "experience" of that data.

If this idea seems farfetched, consider its current applications at the boundaries between art and mathematics. Stewart Dickson and Michael Scroggins

Figure 5.15 **Network Visualization of the Structure of World Trade.** Imagine this display as a virtual reality display. Imagine moving around inside this dense forest of spheres and lines, "experiencing the data."

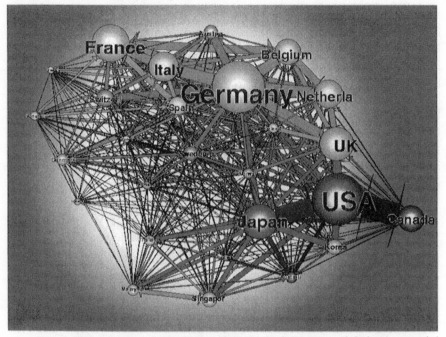

Source: Lothar Krempel, "Structures of World Trade," www.mpi-fg-koeln.mpg.de/ ~lk/netvis/trade/WorldTrade.html. Reprinted with permission.

have teamed together to design the Topological Slide (Figure 5.16). This is a virtual reality display that features a tiltable platform as the main interface. A user steps onto the platform, with the requisite headmounted display, and by shifting his body position is able to simulate "surfing" through the virtual space. Scroggins wished to avoid obvious physical analogies like skiing or wave surfing, which he believed would degenerate into a kind of "VR karaoke where one could replace Frankie and Annette as surfing heroes." Instead, the two wished to explore the idea of surfing—they prefer the word "sliding"— in an abstract space. "An attempt to recuperate some aspect of the surfing model," recalls Scroggins, "led me to consider utilizing the continuous loop- ing flow of a Mobius strip as a substitute for a simulated wave." Dickson suggested the idea of surfing non-Euclidian surfaces, which appealed to Scroggins, whose own "modernist indoctrination gave weight to the idea that traversing mathematical objects was much more interesting than riding a weak replica of an ocean wave."[36]

Beyond artistic interest, this application is important for epistemological

Figure 5.16 **Topological Slide**. By shifting his body position on a tiltable platform, a user is able to simulate "surfing" through an abstract mathematical space, in this case an Enneper's Surface. Sliding inside abstract space makes that space seem tangible and physical, and thus amenable to direct—albeit virtual—experience, as a spelunker might explore a cavern. That is, virtual reality data spaces suggest a different relationship between the user and the data. Instead of observing a diagram from an objective and voyeuristic distance, flying around and inside that diagram would be empathetic and exploratory. Exploration and understanding are thus united; the virtual reality application would allow for an empathetic "feel for the abstract data."

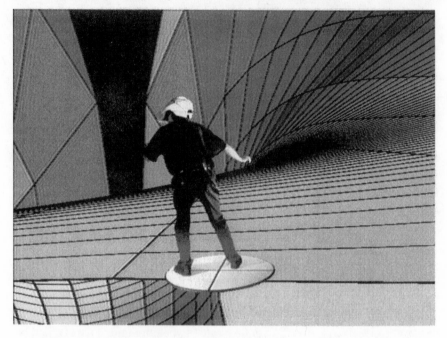

Source: Michael Scroggins, "Topological Slide: Introduction," emsh.calarts.edu/~aka/topological_slide/Introduction.html. Reprinted with permission.

reasons. "Experiencing the abstract-made-concrete," observed Scroggins, "was clearly a more valuable process than experiencing the actual-made-virtual." Sliding inside abstract space makes that space seem tangible and physical, and thus amenable to direct—albeit virtual—experience. A virtual reality environment allows the user to explore this abstract space of concepts as a spelunker might explore a cavern. That is, virtual reality data spaces suggest a different relationship between the user and the data. Instead of observing a diagram from an objective and voyeuristic distance, flying around and inside that diagram would be empathetic and exploratory. "In addition to the sensual delight of navigating the surfaces in a very physical way," writes Scroggins, "I wanted to gain an understanding of the principles by which those surfaces are formed and the underlying concepts that make them interesting to mathematicians."[37] Exploration and understanding are thus united; in the same way the botanist Barbara McClintock spoke of an empathetic "feel for the organism," the virtual reality application would allow for an empathetic "feel for the abstract data."

By navigating around and through the space, the viewer shifts perspectives, which suggests other implications for how we might understand abstract conceptual data. Imagine our flight through the structure of world trade, first from an objective distance, then circling around the outside, then sailing into the thickets of links, only to alight on top of one of the spheres. From each of the different vantage points, the shape of the data will appear different, thus making point of view an integral part of the data exploration. Unlike a traditional chart or diagram—which is limited to a single vantage point at some "distance" from the viewer—a virtual data space is not fixed at some point, but is rather a collection of vantage points; the vantage point from which we choose to view that data will have important effects on the meaning of that data. To a viewer observing the structure of world trade from afar, the information has different meaning from someone surrounded by the tangles of links between nodes. Our understanding of the data is shaped by our physical point of view and the resulting vista, very much in the same way that our historiographic point of view shapes our interpretation of primary sources.

Scroggins and Dickson treat mathematical objects as if they were real tangible objects, like abstract objets d'art. "There is a long and rich history to the linkage of art and mathematics," notes Scroggins. "One way of thinking of [Topological Slide] is to consider the topological surfaces as priori objects presented as art. Jung remarked that numbers might be seen to be as much discovered as invented by man, and Duchamp established that the found object could take on a power equivalent to that of the crafted art object."[38] There are important implications to thinking of virtual reality simulations of abstract conceptual spaces as art objects.

For instance, what if instead of virtual objects, a technology were employed that made these abstract data sculptures into real physical sculptures? Dickson, a sculptor by training, has been especially interested in stereolithography, a technology that turns abstract shapes into tangible objects. Stereolithography is a "computer-aided prototyping technology." This technology takes three-dimensional representations of shapes on a computer screen and "carves" them into physical objects. This technology, explains Dickson, "uses a liquid polymer resin which hardens when exposed to ultraviolet light. Like a three-dimensional laser printer, the apparatus deposits successive layers of hardened material one upon another. Each layer is a successive two-dimensional cross-section of the three dimensional database which has been calculated in the computer."[39] Stereolithography is chiefly employed by engineering and design firms, whose ideas on the screen can be converted to simple prototypes much more quickly than traditional hand-built models.

Dickson, who as we noted above has been interested in the artistic and aesthetic dimensions of mathematics, weds stereolithography to topography.[40] He uses a common mathematics software package to design complex shapes, then converts these into liquid resin form. "I have programmed the interfaces necessary to allow Stereolithography to render the abstract mathematical statement in three-dimensional figures that you can touch and hold." Not unlike the application of virtual reality to abstract shape, this technique suggests a different way to experience abstraction in concrete form, "a more immediate experience of the higher-dimensional abstraction" found in mathematics.[41] Dickson envisions a future where "rather than looking at a computer screen to visualize a scientific model, you'll be able to press a button and walk away with a physical model. It's interesting to speculate what this capacity would do for both science and art"[42] and, we might add, history.

Dickson is not interested simply in aesthetics; far from creating decorative affectation or illustration, manufacturing tangible objects from abstract form is a way to achieve scientific understanding. "A physical stereolithography model can help researchers understand a complicated mathematical surface better than a picture of it on a two-dimensional screen. They can hold a model at any angle, and even place their fingers into the nooks and crannies. I would assume that [these] models would be quite useful for blind people attempting to understand mathematical surfaces"[43] or any such abstract shape of data. As with virtual reality, understanding here involves shifting points of view and multiple perspectives and vistas. It also includes the introduction of the tactile experience of shape and form. If historians were to apply this technology to their three-dimensional abstract visualizations of world trade or gift exchange, what would that historical information feel like?

If the idea of a physical sculpture as a representation of the past seems outrageous, consider historical monuments, which are efforts to give visual, tangible shape to the past. Granted, many historical monuments are representative likenesses of individuals intended to commemorate heroism and are thus not strictly "scholarly." However, some aim to give shape to multivariate abstract ideas and concepts in a way scholars might find more legitimate. Take the Vietnam Memorial in Washington, D.C. That sculpture is an abstract chronology of the names of the soldiers who died in the conflict, as well as a graphic form of that chronology. As with any other visualization, a viewer can discern both whole and part relationships between the data. As one enters the monument, the number of casualties is small and the viewer towers over the monument, which does not rise above the level of one's knees. The viewer then follows the chronology by walking alongside the stone walls of the monument. The viewer sees the war escalating by noting that the number of names increases. The black stone that holds the names now towers over the viewer, who is soon overwhelmed by the weight of the loss of life. Near the end, the viewer experiences American involvement scaling back, since the number of names decreases and the monument shrinks back to knee-level. Edward Tufte remarks that the memorial conveys three dimensions of data: a memorialization of the people killed in the war, the physical marks of the names which shape the entire memorial, and a sequence and chronology of the war.[44] This experience is like moving through a virtual reality datascape, only in this case the data are tangible and real.

This complex, multidimensional abstract sculpture could serve as a model for how historians might use sterolithography to create tangible sculptures of our abstract three-dimensional concept maps of the past. While they need not be as monumental as the Vietnam Memorial, our digital sculptures could nevertheless serve as ways for viewers to think about the past by directly experiencing the shape of events, by moving around and observing the data from different angles, even by touching the data. Like the Venus figures of the Neolithic, stereolithic visualizations give tangible shape to ideas.

Publication

These technologies and applications are not science fiction; they exist right now and are already being put to use in other disciplines. Yet historians are still some distance away from producing similar abstract models of their data and interpretations, for the simple reason that most of us have not been trained to do so. Further, for most practicing historians, there is little incentive to create such visual models. Since our profession does not consider abstract data models to be legitimate forms of publication, few aspiring academic historians would dare risk their hiring prospects or tenure chances on such risky ventures.

The profession's concerns over the legitimacy of nonwritten models as publishable secondary sources are reasonable and necessary. There are concerns about the intellectual rigor of visualizations, concerns that I hope to have alleviated in the course of this book. In addition, we have not yet developed evaluative standards for assessing the credibility, reliability, and legitimacy of any publication venues that might display abstract visual models. As a result, abstract visualizations, GIS displays, virtual reality simulations, data sculptures, or, indeed, any other sorts of visual/spatial secondary sources do not yet have institutionally recognized sites for publication. Only when historians develop procedures for establishing the quality and validity of these sites can we expect abstract visual secondary sources to flourish. This is not to suggest, of course, that there will not be those who flood cyberspace with abstract visualizations claiming them to be "historical," in the same way writers writing of the past or filmmakers filming the past claim their works to be historical. Creating and sustaining these publication havens must occur first before they can be filled with visual models used by historians as tools of scholarly expression and communication.

There is no reason why our traditional publication venues could not be re-worked to accommodate abstract visualizations. A good place to start is with the Ph.D. Advisers and dissertation committees might begin to accept a GIS display, a data mining visualization, or an abstract data sculpture as a legiti-mate research project. Just as art students must produce a portfolio of their work or produce a show or exhibition as a major requirement for an advanced degree, graduate students in history might similarly produce a collection of their visual secondary sources. The committee would need to determine crite-ria of rigor for abstract visualizations, then allow their students to submit these in lieu of the traditional dissertation. (Less adventuresome students might sub-mit the visualization in addition to a written account, but that written account would be only a supplement, not the main vehicle.) I once suggested to a team of graduate students who had produced a GIS display as a conference presen-tation that if they were my students I would accept a more rigorous version of their display as the equivalent of a dissertation. Their reaction spoke volumes: they were at once thrilled with the idea, but also skeptical of the chances of their committees actually agreeing to such a radical suggestion.

Once a critical mass of such visually trained graduate students matricu-late, they will then have to spread out into the profession before abstract visualizations become a common part of our professional life. In discerning the qualifications of a candidate, hiring committees would need to establish procedures of evaluation to judge a visual dissertation. Such evaluation pro-cedures would need to accord the visualization the same weight and legiti-macy as a traditional written dissertation before visual models can ever begin to be used as evidence for suitability for employment. This raises, of course, a classic chicken-and-egg issue: the number of visual historians hired will increase only when sympathetic historians are in leadership positions where they can hire visual historians to eventually serve in leadership positions to hire visual historians.

Once hired, the historian could use the traditional journal, or at least its digital equivalent, as a legitimate site for publishing abstract visualizations.

In a traditional print journal, static abstract visualizations might be published alongside more traditional prose articles—for example, an analysis of gift exchange patterns shaped as a multivariate, data-rich concept map. These visualizations would be something like academic "charticles"; that is, the visualization would be the main "article" and any written prose would serve as the supplement to that visualization. An on-line or electronic journal could very easily accommodate abstract visualizations, with the added benefit of permitting animation. Historiographic forums—that is, visualizations reflecting different interpretations of the same information—could be organized by placing different visualizations alongside one another, thus allowing viewers to compare, contrast, and debate the different forms produced by historians. Note that this idea of publishing abstract visualizations does not mean simply adding more visual materials to illustrate written articles. The visualizations themselves would be the articles.

Historians might also exhibit their abstract visualizations at conferences. Rather than reading a paper, the historian would present a visual display. After some explanatory remarks by the designer, the rest of the presentation could be given over to a question-and-answer session. This would not be the same as a presentation with visual aids; like a charticle, the visualization would be the main focus of the presentation. In fact, I imagine such sessions would be more quiet than most presentations, the room silent as viewers observe the visualization, murmuring among themselves like patrons in an art gallery. Like a traditional conference presentation, the visualization could be displayed on large screens, something like an "information mural."[45] Robert Horn describes these as wall-sized information displays, which he uses for business presentations and planning sessions. It is also possible that specially fitted rooms could be made available for these displays. The virtual reality spaces described in the previous chapter could also be used here, especially for virtual reality datascapes.

This visual presentation need not be so grand, of course. It might be easier to display the visualization on a screen or terminal and have viewers walk by and ask questions at their leisure, something like a poster session. While this is a common practice in other disciplines, historians generally do not include poster sessions at their professional meetings because they are generally not perceived to be as prestigious or as rigorous as a paper presentation. A poster session, however, would seem a natural forum for abstract visualizations. Peer review procedures could be easily applied to these presentations, making it easier to accord a visual display the same status as a conference paper or even a published paper. In any event, here is a case where a change in our thinking about traditional venues of publication would admit visual secondary sources into our profession on the same footing as a prose article.

One could also use a poster session format to display data sculptures. Instead of computer terminals, viewers would observe three-dimensional models of data constructed via sterolithography, as if they were strolling in a sculpture garden. Imagine historians examining similar Brancusi-like data sculptures with titles like "Fall of Rome" or "The Network of World Trade, 1981–1992." Whole "panels" could be given over to the models of different historians, each with their own interpretation of the data, or such panels could be devoted to the work of one historian, making them de facto "exhibitions." As in the art world, having such an exhibition would be a mark of distinction for the designer; historians could also claim on their vita that they were honored with a show of their work at a major conference, claiming this as evidence of first-rate scholarly "publication." These models might also be constructed in larger, more monumental sizes. Like a sculpture by Henry Moore, an historian's abstract data sculpture might be permanently displayed in some outdoor venue. In this case, the data sculpture could serve as a type of large-scale abstract visualization, something like the Vietnam Memorial.

If the above examples seem abstract and esoteric, at some distance from the past they are supposed to model, recall that a page of prose resides at a similar distance from the past it models. Prose compositions are not "the past" but a constructed representation of the past, designed by an historian. The cognitive leap from an abstract page of prose to an abstract space of symbols is not as far as we might imagine. Rather than using computers to construct history as a line of words, historians might instead use computers to form history into a multidimensional shape.

Conclusion

The nineteenth-century novel *Flatland* provides a useful analogy for thinking about the differences between prose and visualizations. In that novel, A. Square, an inhabitant of a two-dimensional world called Flatland, dreams of a visit to a one-dimensional world called Lineland. Lineland is governed by a monarch, who oversees the daily activities of its citizens. These citizens are line segments of varying length who go about their business in a perfectly ordinary fashion, marrying, raising families, and the like. "It seemed that this poor ignorant Monarch," recounts A. Square, "was persuaded that the Straight Line which he called his Kingdom, and in which he passed his existence, constituted the whole of the world, and indeed the whole of Space. Not being able to move or to see, save in his Straight Line, he had no conception of anything outside it. . . . Outside his World, or Line, all was a blank to him; nay, not even a blank, for a blank implies Space; say, rather, all was non-existent."[1] A. Square pities the monarch his limited existence, marvels at the odd shape of his society, and then attempts to explain the concept of "width" to the king without success. The monarch neither comprehends this world A. Square describes nor finds his own universe particularly pitiable or odd. A. Square, from his vantage point, sees the limitations that the monarch, confined to his one dimension, cannot.

A. Square is then visited by A. Sphere, an inhabitant of three-dimensional Spaceland. Like the monarch of Lineland, A. Square cannot conceive of another dimension beyond length and width; "height" has no meaning for him. The inhabitants of Flatland lead perfectly ordinary lives and do not perceive any problems with the arrangement of their world. Failing to convince A. Square of the existence of three dimensions via the analogy of Lineland, A. Sphere plucks A. Square out of his dimension, allowing him to see Flatland from a new perspective and thus to understand the limitations of his two-dimensional world.

Written prose is like an object from Lineland. Since historians think through prose, the past appears to us as a one-dimensional line. Unaware of any other rigorous idiom of thought or communication, historians find it difficult to see the limitations of the medium, for prose serves our needs just fine. Like the inhabitants of Lineland who carry on a perfectly normal existence, we insist that prose serves as a perfectly useful model of the past. Once we learn of the existence of two- and three-dimensional visualizations, however, we might then understand the limitations of prose. But note, like the world of Lineland, prose is not pitiable, only bounded and limited.

Thomas Carlyle understood these limitations without leaving the Lineland of prose. He recognized the difficulties of using a one-dimensional medium to describe a multidimensional reality even if he did not conceive of another idiom through which to model that reality. I would suggest that contemporary historians who, like Carlyle, recognize the limitations of prose and who seek to "escape Lineland" might find visualizations a useful way to think about and model the multidimensionality of the past.

Hayden White reminds us that historians work with models and asks us to think carefully about the formal structural properties of our models. In this book, I have asked historians to similarly examine the structural properties of writing and visualizations as forms of historical models. Both a page of prose and a visualization are simplified replicas of the world they attempt to capture. Both involve symbols and syntax, the meaningful arrangement of those symbols. The differences between the two forms have much to do with the dimensionality of this syntax. Prose is a type of one-dimensional linear model. The symbols of this model—words—have limited degrees of syntactic freedom, in that they must line up in sequence. Like an inhabitant of Lineland, a writer of prose has only one choice of where to place the next word in the sequence. There is no choice of "width" in prose, yet the writer of prose goes about his work just fine. The value of prose lies in its ability to reduce and simplify multidimensionality into one-dimensional chains. Prose enables analysis, the ability to see parts before wholes. For historians, prose allows us to view the past as a sentence.

A visualization, on the other hand, is a type of multidimensional model, in that the symbols—words, shapes, objects, colors—enjoy wider degrees of syntactic freedom. The designer of a visualization may arrange these symbols within a web of connections. Symbols connect in length and width and even in height. The value of a visualization lies in its ability to expand to fill the multidimensional reality in which we live, allowing for synthesis, the understanding of wholes before parts. Historians who use visualizations might begin to think of the past as an architecture.

As I have stated throughout this book, visualizations are useful models of historical scholarship not because they are decorative and eye-catching. They are not merely supplements to written prose nor are they a convenient way for "visual learners" to acquire information. They are not just for school-children, museum patrons, or history buffs. They do not make the past "come to life." Visualizations are useful models for historical scholarship because of their ability to shape our thoughts, to model more of the multidimensionality of the past, and to clearly communicate this understanding to a scholarly audience.

Unlike the blissfully unaware monarch of Lineland, historians now have a choice for how we may model the past. Those choices open up to us once we recognize the validity of other idioms of thought and communication. The computer has made these choices easier to identify, for the computer is an excellent technology for visual thinking. In the Kunstkammern of human history, the computer does not belong next to the printing press. Rather, it belongs next to the telescope, the microscope, and other technologies that have enabled humans to "see" more of the world. Historians who have yet to "escape Lineland" may one day soon recognize the value of the computer not as a fancy word processor but as a digital canvas.

Why should historians make this cognitive leap? Why model the past in two or three dimensions? Why think of the past as a shape rather than as a line? What is wrong with prose? As I have maintained throughout this book, describing the world in sequence is perfectly fine; I have chosen to do so myself, as this book attests. But writers of prose should think sequentially without illusion—that is, we must not allow sequence to blind us to the possibilities of multidimensionality. As Edward Tufte observes, "all the interesting worlds (physical, biological, imaginary, human) that we seek to understand are inevitably and happily multivariate in nature."[2] The past is one such interesting multivariate and multidimensional world.

Notes

Chapter 1. Prose and History

1. Thomas Carlyle, "On History," in Fritz Stern, ed., *The Varieties of History: From Voltaire to the Present* (New York: Vintage Books, 1972), 95.

2. Hayden White, *Metahistory: The Historical Imagination in Nineteenth-Century Europe* (Baltimore: Johns Hopkins University Press, 1973), 2 (emphasis in original).

3. Ibid., 1–42.

4. Robert A. Rosenstone, "Editorial," *World History Bulletin* (Fall 1997): 16–19.

5. Michael Stanford, *The Nature of Historical Knowledge* (Oxford: Basil Blackwell, 1986), 130, 142.

6. Hayden White, "Historiography and Historiophoty," *American Historical Review* 93 (December 1988): 1193–1199.

7. See Robert A. Rosenstone, *Visions of the Past: The Challenge of Film to Our Idea of History* (Cambridge: Harvard University Press, 1995).

8. G.W.F Hegel, *The Philosophy of History*, trans. J. Sibree (New York: Dover Publications, 1956), 1, 2.

9. Ibid., 60.

10. Ibid., 2.

11. Ivan Illich and Barry Sanders, *The Alphabetization of the Popular Mind* (San Francisco: North Point Press, 1988), 3.

12. Victor Papanek, *Design for the Real World: Human Ecology and Social Change* (Chicago: Academy Chicago Publishers, 1984), 1.

13. See David J. Staley, "Designing and Displaying Historical Information in the Electronic Age," *AHA Perspectives* 36 (December 1998): 40–44.

14. Steven Pinker, *The Language Instinct: How the Mind Creates Language* (New York: Harper Perennial, 1994), 56, 57–58.

15. See Howard Gardner, *Frames of Mind: The Theory of Multiple Intelligences* (New York: Basic Books, 1983).

16. Howard Gardner, "Reflections on Multiple Intelligences: Myths and Messages." *Phi Delta Kappan* 77 (November 1995): 200–209.

17. The idea of "essence" comes from Douglas R. Hofstadter, *Le Ton beau de Marot: In Praise of the Music of Language* (New York: Basic Books, 1997), 171–232.

18. See Jay David Bolter, *Writing Space: The Computer, Hypertext and the History of Writing* (Hillsdale, NJ: Lawrence Erlbaum Associates, 1991).

19. For a useful introduction, see Steven Pinker, *Words and Rules: The Ingredients of Language* (New York: Basic Books, 1999).

20. Rosenstone, *Visions of the Past*, 70.

21. Douglas R. Hofstadter, *Godel, Escher, Bach: An Eternal Golden Braid* (New York: Vintage Books, 1979), 90.

22. Hofstadter, *Le Ton beau de Marot*, 305.

23. Edward T. Hall, *Beyond Culture* (New York: Doubleday, 1981), 91.

24. Roderick Floud, *An Introduction to Quantitative Methods for Historians* (London: Methuen, 1973), 4.

25. See, for instance, Jerry P. King, *The Art of Mathematics* (New York: Fawcett Columbine, 1992).

26. For a detailed comparison between numerical symbols and words, see Jacques Barzun and Henry F. Graff, *The Modern Researcher*, 4th ed. (New York: Harcourt Brace Jovanovich, 1985), 150–151.

27. Mitchell Stephens, *The Rise of the Image, The Fall of the Word* (New York: Oxford University Press, 1998), 63.

28. Marshall McLuhan, *Understanding Media: The Extensions of Man* (New York: McGraw-Hill, 1964), 85.

29. Rudolf Arnheim, *Visual Thinking* (Berkeley: University of California Press, 1969), 246.

30. John Kissick, *Art: Context and Criticism* (London: Brown & Benchmark, 1996), 58.

31. McLuhan, 85, 86.

32. Perhaps historians are unconsciously drawn to writing because writing is a medium structured in time—that is, words unfold in time. Since historians see their discipline as one which deals with time, perhaps we believe that writing best captures the essence of time.

33. McLuhan, 85.

34. See Leonard Shlain, *The Alphabet versus the Goddess: The Conflict Between Word and Image* (New York: Viking, 1998).

35. Betty Edwards, *Drawing on the Artist Within* (New York: Fireside, 1986), 95.

36. For an introduction to hypertextual theory, see George P. Landow, *Hypertext: The Convergence of Contemporary Critical Theory and Technology* (Baltimore: Johns Hopkins University Press, 1992); and Bolter, *Writing Space.*

37. Cited in Bolter, 159.

38. Landow, 87.

39. Ibid.

40. Arnheim, 232.

41. Bolter, 127.

42. Ibid., 128–129.

Chapter 2. Visualization As an Alternative to Prose

1. Horst Bredekamp, *The Lure of Antiquity and the Cult of the Machine: The Kunstkammer and the Evolution of Nature, Art and Technology.* (Princeton, NJ: Markus Wiener Publishers, 1995), 113.

2. Quoted in Stephen Eick, "What Is Information Visualization?" n.d. www.bell-labs.com/user/eick/bibliography/1977/toward/node2.html (March 1999).

3. Alexander Stille, "The Betrayal of History," *New York Review of Books*, June 11, 1998, 15.

4. William Draves, *How to Teach Adults in One Hour* (Manhattan, KS: Learning Resource Network, 1984), 23.

5. Robert Lucky, *Silicon Dreams: Information, Man, and Machine* (New York: St. Martin's Press, 1989), 296–297.

6. On the importance of visual thinking to general education, see Rudolf Arnheim, *Thoughts on Art Education* (Los Angeles: Getty Center for Education in the Arts, 1989); and *Visual Thinking* (Berkeley: University of California Press, 1969), 294–315; Betty Edwards, *Drawing on the Artist Within* (New York: Fireside, 1986); and *Drawing on the Right Side of the Brain* (New York: Tarcher/Putnam, 1999).

7. Kathryn Henderson, *On Line and On Paper: Visual Representations, Visual Culture, and Computer Graphics in Design Engineering* (Cambridge, MA: MIT Press, 1999), vii.

8. Vincent Ercolano, "Seeing Is Achieving," *ASEE Prism* (December 1995): 29–31; Beverly Gimmestad Baartmans and Sheryl A. Sorby, *Introduction to 3–D Spatial Visualization* (Englewood Cliffs, NJ: Prentice Hall, 1996).

9. James Elkins, *The Domain of Images* (Ithaca, NY: Cornell University Press, 1999).

10. Elkins, 4–6; cited in Edward Tufte, *Envisioning Information* (Cheshire, CT: Graphics Press, 1990), 9.

11. Elkins, 40.

12. Eick, op. cit. (emphasis added).

13. Stephen Hall, *Mapping the Next Millennium* (New York: Vintage, 1992), 247–264.

14. See Henry Mintzberg and Ludo Van der Heyden, "Organigraphs: Drawing How Companies Really Work," *Harvard Business Review* (September–October 1999): 87–94.

15. Alfred Crosby, *The Measure of Reality: Quantification and Western Society, 1250–1600* (Cambridge, MA: Cambridge University Press, 1997), 144.

16. Edward Rothstein, *Emblems of Mind: The Inner Life of Music and Mathematics* (New York: Times Books/Random House, 1994), 18.

17. Wassily Kandinsky, *Point and Line to Plane* (New York: Dover Publications, 1979), 83.

18. Steven R. Holtzman, *Digital Mantras: The Languages of Abstract and Virtual Worlds* (Cambridge, MA: MIT Press, 1994), 269.

19. Donis A. Dondis, *A Primer of Visual Literacy* (Cambridge, MA: MIT Press, 1973), 182.

20. Ellen Lupon, "Visual Dictionary," in Ellen Lupon and J. Abbott Miller, eds., *The ABC's of Bauhaus: The Bauhaus and Design Theory* (Princeton, NJ: Princeton Architectural Press, 1991), 22–33.

21. See Robert E. Horn, *Visual Language: Global Communication for the 21st Century* (Bainbridge Island, WA: MacroVu, 1998), 65.

22. Christopher Alexander, et al. *A Pattern Language* (New York: Oxford University Press, 1977).

23. Cited in Arnheim, *Visual Thinking*, 234.

24. This example derives from Arnheim, *Visual Thinking*, 235.

25. A useful introduction, marred by too much emphasis on decoration, is Jan V. White, *Using Charts and Graphs: 1000 Ideas for Visual Persuasion* (New York: Bowker, 1984), 6.

26. Donald Weismann, *The Visual Arts as Human Experience* (New York: Prentice-Hall, 1970), 11.

27. Barbara Maria Stafford, *Visual Analogy: Consciousness as the Art of Connecting* (Cambridge, MA: MIT Press, 1999), 9.

28. Ibid., 169.

29. See Monty Newborn, *Kasparov versus Deep Blue: Computer Chess Comes of Age* (New York: Springer-Verlag New York, 1997), 69. Douglas Hofstadter has long been fascinated with this property of human intelligence and the ability to program computers to make analogies. See Hofstadter, *Fluid Concepts and Creative Analogies: Computer Models of the Fundamental Mechanisms of Thought* (New York: Basic Books, 1995).

30. Horn, 111.

31. Edward Tufte, *The Visual Display of Quantitative Information* (Cheshire, CT: Graphics Press, 1983), 13.

32. Ibid., 91–105.

33. Ibid., 107–121.

34. Stafford, 9.

35. See Marshall Sahlins, *Islands of History* (Chicago: University of Chicago Press, 1985), 144.

36. Cited in Niall Ferguson, ed., *Virtual History: Alternatives and Counterfactuals* (New York: Basic Books, 1999), 64.

37. Ibid., 58 (emphasis added).

Chapter 3. Visual Secondary Sources

1. Freeman J. Dyson, *The Sun, the Genome, and the Internet: Tools of Scientific Revolutions* (New York: Oxford University Press, 1999), xiv.

2. Paul Krugman, *Development, Geography, and Economic Theory* (Cambridge, MA: MIT Press, 1995), 69–70.

3. Cited in Robert A. Rosenstone, *Visions of the Past: The Challenge of Film to Our Idea of History* (Cambridge, MA: Harvard University Press, 1995),133.

4. Michael E. Hobart and Zachary S. Schiffman, *Information Ages: Literacy, Numeracy, and the Computer Revolution* (Baltimore: Johns Hopkins University Press, 1998), 5.

5. Francis Haskell, *History and Its Images: Art and the Interpretation of the Past* (New Haven, CT: Yale University Press, 1993), 1–2.

6. For a definition of proxemics, see Edward T. Hall, *The Hidden Dimension* (New York: Doubleday, 1966), 1.

7. See for example Peter Burke, *Eyewitnessing: The Uses of Images as Historical Evidence* (Ithaca, NY: Cornell University Press, 2001); and Raphael Samuel, *Theatres of Memory* (London: Verso, 1994).

8. For an interesting example of what I mean by a quaternary source, see Richard J. Evans, *In Defense of History* (New York: W.W. Norton, 1999).

9. Great care must be taken when displaying visual primary sources. Often, textbook publishers—for this decision is rarely made by the author of the (written) text—

will place a visual source within an account in a way that is anachronistic. In one Western civilization textbook, a chapter on the foundations of Judaism featured an image of Moses: Michelangelo's sculpture of Moses, that is. In another account, the publisher included an impressionistic painting of American canals; the caption implied that this was a "picture" of these canals, a representational image. For an example of an excellent use of images as primary sources, see Hagan Schultze, *Germany: A New History* (Cambridge, MA: Harvard University Press, 1998).

10. Vincent Virga, *Eyes of the Nation: A Visual History of the United States* (New York: Alfred A. Knopf, 1997).

11. For another fine example, see Peter Menzel, *Material World: A Global Family Portrait* (San Francisco: Sierra Club Books, 1994). I have used this collection in my classes, asking students to see not only what is present but what the photographer "left out."

12. William McNeill, *A World History* (New York: Oxford University Press, 1979), vi.

13. John Berger, *Ways of Seeing* (London: BBC and Penguin, 1972), 6.

14. Tyler Volk, *Metapatterns: Across Space, Time and Mind* (New York: Columbia University Press, 1995).

15. See "Paradise Found and Lost: Migration in the Ohio Valley 1850–1970," a permanent display located at the Campus Martius Museum in Marietta, Ohio. The display won the 1998 Public History Award from the Ohio Academy of History.

16. See Gary Kulik, "Designing the Past: History-Museum Exhibitions from Peale to the Present," in Warren Leon and Roy Rosenzweig, eds., *History Museums in the United States: A Critical Assessment* (Urbana: University of Illinois Press, 1989), 3–37. See also Steven Conn, *Museums and American Intellectual Life, 1876–1926* (Chicago: University of Chicago Press, 1998).

17. See Gaynor Kavanagh, ed., *Museum Languages: Objects and Texts* (Leicester, UK: Leicester University Press, 1991); and Eilean Hooper-Greenhill, ed., *Museum, Media, Message* (London: Routledge, 1995).

18. Kulik, 12.

19. See Horst Bredekamp, *The Lure of Antiquity and the Cult of the Machine: The Kunstkammer and the Evolution of Nature, Art and Technology* (Princeton, NJ: Markus Wiener, 1995).

20. David Mamet, *On Directing Film* (New York: Penguin Books, 1991), 5.

21. Rosenstone, 11, 15.

22. See Tony Horwitz, *Confederates in the Attic: Dispatches from the Unfinished Civil War* (New York: Pantheon Books, 1998).

23. Denis Wood, *The Power of Maps* (New York: Guilford Press, 1992), 42–43.

24. Jeremy Black, *Maps and History: Constructing Images of the Past* (New Haven, CT: Yale University Press, 1997), 27–50.

25. Wood, 1.

26. See Mark Monmonier, *Mapping It Out: Expository Cartography for the Humanities and Social Sciences* (Chicago: University of Chicago Press, 1993).

27. Elizabeth Hill Boone, "Aztec Pictorial Histories: Records without Words," in Elizabeth Hill Boone and Walter D. Mignolo, eds., *Writing Without Words: Alternative Literacies in Mesoamerica and the Andes* (Durham, NC: Duke University Press, 1994), 60–68.

28. H.G. Wells, *The Outline of History: Being a Plain History of Life and Mankind*, 3d ed. (New York: Macmillan, 1921), 1123.

29. Eric Homberger, *The Penguin Historical Atlas of North America* (New York: Viking/Penguin, 1995), 1.

30. Hall, 6.

31. James Elkins, *The Domain of Images* (Ithaca, NY: Cornell University Press, 1999), 258.

32. See David J. Staley, "Visualizing the Relationship between Speech, Writing and Image," *Comparative Civilizations Review* (Spring 1997): 77–98.

Chapter 4. Virtual Reality

1. Janet Murray, *Hamlet on the Holodeck: The Future of Narrative in Cyberspace* (Cambridge, MA: MIT Press, 1997).

2. Anne H. Soukhanov, *Word Watch: The Stories Behind the Words of Our Lives* (New York: Henry Holt, 1995), 315.

3. Ken Pimentel and Kevin Teixeira, *Virtual Reality: Through the New Looking Glass* (New York: Intel/Windcrest/McGraw-Hill, 1993), 33.

4. Mary Anne Moser, ed. *Immersed in Technology: Art and Virtual Environments* (Cambridge, MA: MIT Press, 1996), 207.

5. In addition to Pimentel and Teixeira, see Mark Pesce, *VRML: Browsing and Building Cyberspace* (Indianapolis: New Riders Publishing, 1995); L. Casey Larijan, *The Virtual Reality Primer* (New York: McGraw-Hill, 1994); Howard Rheingold, *Virtual Reality* (New York: Summit Books, 1991).

6. Toni Dove, "Artificial Changelings," n.d. www.funnygarbage.com/dove (May 14, 2002); *Body Mecanique: Artistic Explorations and Digital Realms* (Columbus: Wexner Center for the Arts, The Ohio State University, 1998).

7. Thomas Seebohm, "Computer Assisted Simulation and Design," August 3, 1998, www.fes.uwaterloo.ca/u/tseebohm/home/simulation/vill92–fount.gif (May 14, 2002).

8. "The Lost Museum," 2001, www.lostmuseum.cuny.edu/home.html (May 14, 2002).

9. Foundation of the Hellenic World, "3D Reconstructions: Miletus," n.d., www.fhw.gr/fhw/en/projects/3dvr/miletus/index.html (May 14, 2002).

10. "Virtual Harlem," n.d., evlweb.eecs.uic.edu/cavern/harlem (May 14, 2002).

11. Jeffrey Barlow, "The Buddhist Palace," n.d. mcel.pacificu.edu/omm/ (May 14, 2002).

12. Mary Webb, "Computer-Based Modelling in School History," in Allen Martin, Lez Smart, and David Yeomans, eds., *Information Technology and the Teaching of History: International Perspectives* (Amsterdam: Harwood Academic Publishers, 1997), 213.

13. John Bonnett, "Bringing Students to a Virtual Past: Teaching Ottawa History with the 3–D Historical Cities Project," in Jeff Keshen and Nicole Saint-Onge, eds., *Construire une capitale—Ottawa—Making a Capital* (Ottawa: University of Ottawa Press, 2001), 483–502.

14. Paul Krugman, *Development, Geography, and Economic Theory* (Cambridge, MA: MIT Press, 1995), 71.

15. On the limits of models, see Krugman, 71; Rheingold, 45.

16. Rheingold, 212.

17. Murray, 152.

18. Ibid., 152–153.

19. Ibid., 185, 30.

20. I explore these issues in "Digital Historiography: Subjunctivity," *Journal of the Association for History and Computing* (April 2000) mcel.pacificu.edu/JAHC/JAHCIII1/P-REVIEWS/staleyIII1.html

21. Niall Ferguson, ed., *Virtual History: Alternatives and Counterfactuals* (New York: Basic Books, 1999), 73.

22. Ibid., 87.

23. Ibid., 83.

24. Ibid., 85.

25. Murray, 137.

26. For a discussion of diachronic versus synchronic narrative in history, see Marshall Sahlins, *Islands of History* (Chicago: University of Chicago Press, 1985).

27. Cited in Moser, 275.

28. Murray, 112.

29. See for example Patrick FitzGerald and James Lester, "Knowledge-Based Learning Environments," in Peter H. Martorella, ed., *Interactive Technologies and the Social Studies: Emerging Issues and Applications* (Albany: State University of New York Press, 1997), 123.

Chapter 5. History Takes Shape

1. The term comes from Edward Rothstein, *Emblems of Mind: The Inner Life of Music and Mathematics* (New York: Avon Books, 1995), 4, borrowed from a poem by William Wordsworth. Rothstein uses the term to refer to "the mind's creations."

2. Alan Beyerchen, "Nonlinear Science and the Unfolding of a New Intellectual Vision," *Papers in Comparative Studies* 6 (1989): 27.

3. On the connection between the scientific revolution and cartography, see David W. Livingstone, *The Geographical Tradition: Episodes in the History of a Contested Enterprise* (Oxford: Blackwell, 1992), 32–35.

4. To view a reproduction of the Lorenz Attractor, go to archive.ncsa.uiuc.edu/SCMS/DigLib/stills/0892.hobill.lg.gif

5. James Gleick, *Chaos: Making a New Science* (New York: Viking, 1987), 47.

6. Ibid., 83–118. To view the Mandelbrot set, see Andy Burbanks, "The Mandelbrot Set," October 28, 1996, www.lboro.ac.uk/departments/ma/gallery/mandel/ (May 16, 2002).

7. Douglas Hofstadter, "Mathematical Chaos and Strange Attractors," in *Metamagical Themas: Questing for the Essence of Mind and Pattern* (New York: Basic Books, 1985), 365.

8. Ibid. (emphasis added).

9. Beyerchen, 31.

10. Mark Monmonier, *Mapping It Out: Expository Cartography for the Humanities and Social Sciences* (Chicago: University of Chicago Press, 1993), 9.

11. Michael E. Hobart and Zachary S. Schiffman, *Information Ages: Literacy, Numeracy, and the Computer Revolution* (Baltimore: Johns Hopkins University Press, 1998), 4.

12. Merlin Donald, *Origins of the Modern Mind: Three Stages in the Evolution of Culture and Cognition* (Cambridge, MA: Harvard University Press, 1991), ch. 8. Ernst

Cassirer distinguished humans from other species in that humans surround themselves with a "symbolic system," a cultural screen of symbols humans have erected by which they encounter the world. See Cassirer, *An Essay on Man* (New Haven, CT: Yale University Press, 1944), 24.

13. Hobart and Schiffman, 4.

14. Ibid., 30.

15. Elizabeth Wayland Barber, *Women's Work, The First 20,000 Years: Women, Cloth, and Society in Early Times* (New York: W.W. Norton, 1994), 148–49.

16. Rudolf Arnheim, *Visual Thinking* (Berkeley: University of California Press, 1969), 120–129. The idea to title this chapter "History Takes Shape" came from Arnheim's chapter "Concepts Take Shape."

17. Betty Edwards, *Drawing on the Artist Within* (New York: Fireside, 1986), 67.

18. Arnheim, 134.

19. Robert Darnton, "An Early Information Society: Maps of Paris," February 2000, www.Indiana.edu/~ahr/darnton/maps (May 16, 2002).

20. For a brief but useful introduction, see the U.S. Geological Survey, "Relating Information from Different Sources," April 20, 2001, www.usgs.gov/research/gis/work1.html (May 18, 2002).

21. Ibid.

22. M.J. Kraak and F.J. Ormeling, *Cartography: Visualization of Spatial Data* (Essex, UK: Addison Wesley Longman, 1996), 1–16.

23. J.B. Owens, "GIS and Research on Region Interactions in World History," paper presented at the annual meeting of the World History Association, June 1999, 3.

24. Ibid., 8.

25. Joseph D. Novak, *Learning, Creating and Using Knowledge: Concept Maps as Facilitative Tools in Schools and Corporations* (Mahwah, NJ: Lawrence Erlbaum Associates, 1998), 40.

26. For a representative example, see Tony Buzan, *The Mind Map Book: How to Use Radiant Thinking to Maximize Your Brain's Untapped Potential* (New York: Dutton, 1994).

27. The idea of nodes and arcs comes from a computer science course at the University of Calgary, Software Engineering 611, October 13, 1998, pages.cpsc.ucalgary.ca/~jonesb/seng/611/techniques.html (May 18, 2002).

28. Novak, 22.

29. Ibid., 38.

30. The term "relational" comes from Edwards, 12.

31. Novak, 192.

32. Alaric Dickinson, "Progression in Children's Thinking and Understanding in History," in Allan Martin, Lez Smart, and David Yeomans, eds., *Information Technology and the Teaching of History: International Perspectives* (Amsterdam: Harwood Academic Publishers, 1997), 111–125.

33. Ibid, 115.

34. See Brian R. Gains and Mildred L.G. Shaw, "WebMap: Concept Mapping on the Web," n.d., www.w3.org/Conferences/WWW4/Papers/134 (May 18, 2002).

35. Note that at the time of this writing, one cannot actually click on the cube.

36. Michael Scroggins and Stewart Dickson, "Topological Slide," in Mary Anne Moser, ed., *Immersed in Technology: Art and Virtual Environments* (Cambridge, MA: MIT Press, 1996), 310.

37. Ibid.

38. Ibid.

39. Stewart Dickson, "Forging a Career as a Sculptor from a Career as a Computer Programmer," in Clifford A. Pickover, ed., *Visions of the Future: Art, Technology and Computing in the Twenty-First Century* (New York: St. Martin's Press, 1992), 31–32.

40. For an interesting example of stereolithography, see Carlo H. Sequin and Paul K. Wright, "Rapid Prototyping Interface for 3D Solid Parts," n.d., cs.Berkeley.edu/~sequin/PROJ/sif.html (May 18, 2002).

41. Ibid., 33.

42. Ibid., 40.

43. Ibid.

44. Edward Tufte, *Envisioning Information* (Cheshire, CT: Graphics Press, 1990), 44.

45. Robert E. Horn, *Visual Language: Global Communication for the 21st Century* (Bainbridge Island, WA: MacroVu, 1998), 63–64.

Conclusion

1. Edwin A. Abbott, *Flatland: A Romance of Many Dimensions* (New York: Dover Publications, 1992 [1884]), 44–45.

2. Edward Tufte, *Envisioning Information* (Cheshire, CT: Graphics Press, 1990), 12.

Bibliography

Abbott, Edwin A. *Flatland: A Romance of Many Dimensions*. New York: Dover Publications, 1992 [1884].

Alexander, Christopher, et al. *A Pattern Language*. New York: Oxford University Press, 1977.

Arnheim, Rudolf. *Thoughts on Art Education*. Los Angeles: Getty Center for Education in the Arts, 1989.

———. *Visual Thinking*. Berkeley: University of California Press, 1969.

Baartmans, Beverly Gimmestad, and Sheryl A. Sorby, *Introduction to 3–D Spatial Visualization*. Englewood Cliffs, NJ: Prentice Hall, 1996.

Barber, Elizabeth Wayland. *Women's Work, The First 20,000 Years: Women, Cloth, and Society in Early Times*. New York: W.W. Norton, 1994.

Barlow, Jeffrey. "Buddhist Palace," n.d. mcel.pacificu.edu/omm/ (May 14, 2002).

Barzun, Jacques, and Henry F. Graff. *The Modern Researcher*. 4th ed. New York: Harcourt Brace Jovanovich, 1985.

Berger, John. *Ways of Seeing*. London: BBC and Penguin, 1972.

Beyerchen, Alan. "Nonlinear Science and the Unfolding of a New Intellectual Vision." *Papers in Comparative Studies* 6 (1989): 25–49.

Black, Jeremy. *Maps and History: Constructing Images of the Past*. New Haven, CT: Yale University Press, 1997.

Body Mecanique: Artistic Explorations and Digital Realms. Columbus: Wexner Center for the Arts, The Ohio State University, 1998.

Bolter, Jay David. *Writing Space: The Computer, Hypertext and the History of Writing*. Hillsdale, NJ: Lawrence Erlbaum Associates, 1991.

Bonnett, John. "Bringing Students to a Virtual Past: Teaching Ottawa History with the 3–D Historical Cities Project." In Jeff Keshen and Nicole Saint-Onge, eds., *Construire une capitale—Ottawa—Making a Capital*. Ottawa: University of Ottawa Press, 2001, 483–502.

Boone, Elizabeth Hill. "Aztec Pictorial Histories: Records without Words." In Elizabeth Hill Boone and Walter D. Mignolo, eds. *Writing Without Words: Alternative Literacies in Mesoamerica and the Andes*. Durham, NC: Duke University Press, 1994.

Bredekamp, Horst. *The Lure of Antiquity and the Cult of the Machine: The Kunstkammer and the Evolution of Nature, Art and Technology.* Princeton, NJ: Markus Wiener Publishers, 1995.

Burbanks, Andy. "The Mandelbrot Set," October 28, 1996, www.lboro.ac.uk/departments/ma/gallery/mandel/ (May 16, 2002).

Burke, Peter. *Eyewitnessing: The Uses of Images as Historical Evidence.* Ithaca, NY: Cornell University Press, 2001.

Buzan, Tony. *The Mind Map Book: How to Use Radiant Thinking to Maximize Your Brain's Untapped Potential.* New York: Dutton, 1994.

Carlyle, Thomas. "On History." In Fritz Stern, ed. *The Varieties of History: From Voltaire to the Present.* New York: Vintage Books, 1972.

Cassirer, Ernst. *An Essay on Man.* New Haven, CT: Yale University Press, 1944.

Conn, Steven. *Museums and American Intellectual Life, 1876–1926.* Chicago: University of Chicago Press, 1998.

Crosby, Alfred. *The Measure of Reality: Quantification and Western Society, 1250–1600.* Cambridge, MA: Cambridge University Press, 1997.

Darnton, Robert. "An Early Information Society: Maps of Paris," February 2000, www.Indiana.edu/~ahr/darnton/maps (May 16, 2002).

Dickinson, Alaric. "Progression in Children's Thinking and Understanding in History." In Allan Martin, Lez Smart, and David Yeomans, eds., *Information Technology and the Teaching of History: International Perspectives.* Amsterdam: Harwood Academic Publishers, 1997, 111–125.

Dickson, Stewart. "Forging a Career as a Sculptor from a Career as a Computer Programmer." In Clifford A. Pickover, ed. *Visions of the Future: Art Technology and Computing in the Twenty-first Century.* New York: St. Martin's Press, 1992.

Donald, Merlin. *Origins of the Modern Mind: Three Stages in the Evolution of Culture and Cognition.* Cambridge, MA: Harvard University Press, 1991.

Dondis, Donis A. *A Primer of Visual Literacy.* Cambridge, MA: MIT Press, 1973.

Dove, Toni. "Artificial Changelings," n.d. www.funnygarbage.com/dove (May 14, 2002).

Draves, William. *How to Teach Adults in One Hour.* Manhattan, KS: Learning Resource Network, 1984.

Dyson, Freeman J. *The Sun, the Genome, and the Internet: Tools of Scientific Revolutions.* New York: Oxford University Press, 1999.

Edwards, Betty. *Drawing on the Right Side of the Brain.* New York: Tarcher/Putnam, 1999.

———. *Drawing on the Artist Within.* New York: Fireside, 1986.

Eick, Stephen. "What Is Information Visualization?" n.d. www.bell-labs.com/user/eick/bibliography/1997/toward/node2.html (March 1999).

Elkins, James. *The Domain of Images.* Ithaca, NY: Cornell University Press, 1999.

Ercolano, Vincent. "Seeing Is Achieving," *ASEE Prism* (December 1995): 29–31.

Evans, Richard J. *In Defense of History.* New York: W.W. Norton, 1999.

Ferguson, Niall, ed. *Virtual History: Alternatives and Counterfactuals.* New York: Basic Books, 1999.

FitzGerald, Patrick and James Lester. "Knowledge-Based Learning Environments." In Peter H. Martorella, ed. *Interactive Technologies and the Social Studies: Emerging Issues and Applications.* Albany: State University of New York Press, 1997.

Floud, Roderick. *An Introduction to Quantitative Methods for Historians.* London: Methuen, 1973.

Foundation of the Hellenic World, "3D Reconstructions: Miletus," n.d., www.fhw.gr/fhw/en/projects/3dvr/miletus/index.html (May 14, 2002).

Gains, Brian R., and Mildred L.G. Shaw. "WebMap: Concept Mapping on the Web," n.d. www.w3.org/Conferences/WWW4/Papers/134 (May 18, 2002).

Gardner, Howard. "Reflections on Multiple Intelligences: Myths and Messages." *Phi Delta Kappan* 77 (November 1995): 200–209.

———. *Frames of Mind: The Theory of Multiple Intelligences.* New York: Basic Books, 1983.

Gleick, James. *Chaos: Making a New Science.* New York: Viking, 1987.

Hall, Edward T. *Beyond Culture.* New York: Doubleday, 1981.

———. *The Hidden Dimension.* New York: Doubleday, 1966.

Hall, Stephen. *Mapping the Next Millennium.* New York: Vintage, 1992.

Haskell, Francis. *History and Its Images: Art and the Interpretation of the Past.* New Haven, CT: Yale University Press, 1993.

Hegel, G.W.F. *The Philosophy of History.* Trans. J. Sibree. New York: Dover Publications, 1956.

Henderson, Kathryn. *On Line and On Paper: Visual Representations, Visual Culture, and Computer Graphics in Design Engineering.* Cambridge, MA: MIT Press, 1999.

Hobart, Michael E., and Zachary S. Schiffman. *Information Ages: Literacy, Numeracy, and the Computer Revolution.* Baltimore: Johns Hopkins University Press, 1998.

Hofstadter, Douglas R. *Le Ton beau de Marot: In Praise of the Music of Language.* New York: Basic Books, 1997.

———. *Fluid Concepts and Creative Analogies: Computer Models of the Fundamental Mechanisms of Thought.* New York: Basic Books, 1995.

———. *Metamagical Themas: Questing for the Essence of Mind and Pattern.* New York: Basic Books, 1985.

———. *Godel, Escher, Bach: An Eternal Golden Braid.* New York: Vintage Books, 1979.

Holtzman, Steven. R. *Digital Mantras: The Languages of Abstract and Virtual Worlds.* Cambridge, MA: MIT Press, 1994.

Homberger, Eric. *The Penguin Historical Atlas of North America.* New York: Viking/Penguin, 1995.

Hooper-Greenhill, Eilean, ed. *Museum, Media, Message.* London: Routledge, 1995.

Horn, Robert E. *Visual Language: Global Communication for the 21st Century.* Bainbridge Island, WA: MacroVu, 1998.

Horwitz, Tony. *Confederates in the Attic: Dispatches from the Unfinished Civil War.* New York: Pantheon Books, 1998.

Illich, Ivan, and Barry Sanders. *The Alphabetization of the Popular Mind.* San Francisco: North Point Press, 1988.

Kandinsky, Wassily. *Point and Line to Plane.* New York: Dover Publications, 1979.

Kavanagh, Gaynor, ed. *Museum Languages: Objects and Texts.* Leicester, UK: Leicester University Press, 1991.

King, Jerry P. *The Art of Mathematics.* New York: Fawcett Columbine, 1992.

Kissick, John. *Art: Context and Criticism.* London: Brown & Benchmark, 1996.

Kraak, M.J., and F.J. Ormeling, *Cartography: Visualization of Spatial Data.* Essex, UK: Addison Wesley Longman, 1996.

Krugman, Paul. *Development, Geography, and Economic Theory.* Cambridge, MA: MIT Press, 1995.

Kulik, Gary. "Designing the Past: History-Museum Exhibitions from Peale to the Present." In Warren Leon and Roy Rosenzweig, eds., *History Museums in the United States: A Critical Assessment.* Urbana: University of Illinois Press, 1989: 3–37.

Landow, George P. *Hypertext: The Convergence of Contemporary Critical Theory and Technology.* Baltimore: Johns Hopkins University Press, 1992.

Larijan, L. Casey. *The Virtual Reality Primer.* New York: McGraw-Hill, 1994.

Livingstone, David W. *The Geographical Tradition: Episodes in the History of a Contested Enterprise.* Oxford: Blackwell, 1992.

"The Lost Museum," 2001, www.lostmuseum.cuny.edu/home.html (May 14, 2002).

Lucky, Robert. *Silicon Dreams: Information, Man, and Machine.* New York: St. Martin's Press, 1989, 296–297.

"Visual Dictionary." In Ellen Lupon and J. Abbott Miller, eds. *The ABC's of Bauhaus: The Bauhaus and Design Theory.* Princeton, NJ: Princeton Architectural Press, 1991.

Mamet, David. *On Directing Film.* New York: Penguin Books, 1991.

Martin, Allen, Lez Smart, and David Yeomans, eds. *Information Technology and the Teaching of History: International Perspectives.* Amsterdam: Harwood Academic Publishers, 1997.

Martorella, Peter H. ed. *Interactive Technologies and the Social Studies: Emerging Issues and Applications.* Albany: State University of New York Press, 1997.

McLuhan, Marshall. *Understanding Media: The Extensions of Man.* New York: McGraw-Hill, 1964.

McNeill, William. *A World History.* New York: Oxford University Press, 1979.

———. *The Rise of the West: A History of the Human Community.* Chicago: University of Chicago Press, 1963.

Menzel, Peter. *Material World: A Global Family Portrait.* San Francisco: Sierra Club Books, 1994.

Mintzberg, Henry, and Ludo Van der Heyden, "Organigraphs: Drawing How Companies Really Work," *Harvard Business Review* (September–October 1999): 87–94.

Monmonier, Mark. *Mapping It Out: Expository Cartography for the Humanities and Social Sciences.* Chicago: University of Chicago Press, 1993.

Moser, Mary Anne, ed. *Immersed in Technology: Art and Virtual Environments.* Cambridge, MA: MIT Press, 1996.

Murray, Janet. *Hamlet on the Holodeck: The Future of Narrative in Cyberspace.* Cambridge, MA: MIT Press, 1997.

Newborn, Monty. *Kasparov versus Deep Blue: Computer Chess Comes of Age.* New York: Springer-Verlag New York, 1997.

Novak, Joseph D. *Learning, Creating and Using Knowledge: Concept Maps as Facilitative Tools in Schools and Corporations.* Mahwah, NJ: Lawrence Erlbaum Associates, 1998.

Owens, J.B. "GIS and Research on Region Interactions in World History." Paper presented at the annual meeting of the World History Association, June 1999.

Papanek, Victor. *Design for the Real World: Human Ecology and Social Change.* Chicago: Academy Chicago Publishers, 1984.

Pesce, Mark. *VRML: Browsing and Building Cyberspace.* Indianapolis: New Riders Publishing, 1995.

Pickover, Clifford A. ed. *Visions of the Future: Art, Technology and Computing in the Twenty-First Century.* New York: St. Martin's Press, 1992.

Pimentel, Ken, and Kevin Teixeira, *Virtual Reality: Through the New Looking Glass.* New York: Intel/Windcrest/McGraw-Hill, 1993.

Pinker, Steven. *Words and Rules: The Ingredients of Language.* New York: Basic Books, 1999.

———. *The Language Instinct: How the Mind Creates Language.* New York: Harper Perennial, 1994.

Rheingold, Howard. *Virtual Reality.* New York: Summit Books, 1991.

Rosenstone, Robert A. "Editorial." *World History Bulletin* (Fall 1997): 16–19.

———. *Visions of the Past: The Challenge of Film to Our Idea of History.* Cambridge, MA: Harvard University Press, 1995.

Rothstein, Edward. *Emblems of Mind: The Inner Life of Music and Mathematics.* New York: Avon Books, 1995.

Sahlins, Marshall. *Islands of History.* Chicago: University of Chicago Press, 1985.

Samuel, Raphael. *Theatres of Memory.* London: Verso, 1994.

Schultze, Hagen. *Germany: A New History.* Cambridge, MA: Harvard University Press, 1998.

Scroggins, Michael, and Steward Dickson. "Topological Slide." In Mary Anne Moser, ed. *Immersed in Technology: Art and Virtual Environments.* Cambridge, MA: MIT Press, 1996.

Seebohm, Thomas. "Computer Assisted Simulation and Design," August 3, 1998, www.fes.uwaterloo.ca/u/tseebohm/home/simulation/vill92–fount.gif (May 14, 2002).

Sequin, Carlo H., and Paul K. Wright. "Rapid Prototyping Interface for 3D Solid Parts," n.d. cs.Berkeley.edu/~sequin/PROJ/sif.html (May 18, 2002).

Shlain, Leonard. *The Alphabet versus the Goddess: The Conflict Between Word and Image.* New York: Viking, 1998.

Soukhanov, Anne H. *Word Watch: The Stories Behind the Words of Our Lives.* New York: Henry Holt, 1995.

Stafford, Barbara Maria. *Visual Analogy: Consciousness as the Art of Connecting.* Cambridge, MA: MIT Press, 1999.

Staley, David J. "Digital Historiography: Subjunctivity." *Journal of the Association for History and Computing* (April 2000) mcel.pacificu.edu/JAHC/JAHCIII1/P-REVIEWS/staleyIII1.html

———. "From Writing to Associative Assemblages: 'History' in an Electronic Culture." In Dennis A. Trinkle, ed., *Writing, Teaching and Researching History in the Electronic Age: History and Computers.* Armonk, NY: M.E. Sharpe, 1998, 3–13.

———. "Designing and Displaying Historical Information in the Electronic Age," *AHA Perspectives* 36 (December 1998): 40–44.

———. "Visualizing the Relationship between Speech, Writing and Image," *Comparative Civilizations Review* (Spring 1997): 77–98.

Stanford, Michael. *The Nature of Historical Knowledge.* Oxford: Basil Blackwell, 1986.

Stephens, Mitchell. *The Rise of the Image, the Fall of the Word.* New York: Oxford University Press, 1998.

Stille, Alexander. "The Betrayal of History." *New York Review of Books,* June 11, 1998, p. 15.

Tufte, Edward. *Envisioning Information.* Cheshire, CT: Graphics Press, 1990.

———. *The Visual Display of Quantitative Information.* Cheshire, CT: Graphics Press, 1983.

U.S. Geological Survey. "Relating Information from Different Sources," April 20, 2001, www.usgs.gov/research/gis/work1.html (May 18, 2002).

Virga, Vincent. *Eyes of the Nation: A Visual History of the United States*. New York: Alfred A. Knopf, 1997.

"Virtual Harlem," n.d., evlweb.eecs.uic.edu/cavern/harlem (May 14, 2002).

Volk, Tyler. *Metapatterns: Across Space, Time and Mind*. New York: Columbia University Press, 1995.

Webb, Mary. "Computer-Based Modelling in School History." In Allen Martin, Lez Smart, and David Yeomans, eds. *Information Technology and the Teaching of History*. Amsterdam: Harwood Academic Publishers, 1997.

Weismann, Donald. *The Visual Arts as Human Experience*. New York: Prentice-Hall, 1970.

Wells, H.G. *The Outline of History: Being a Plain History of Life and Mankind*, 3d ed. New York: Macmillan, 1921.

White, Hayden. *Metahistory: The Historical Imagination in Nineteenth-Century Europe*. Baltimore: Johns Hopkins University Press, 1973.

———. "Historiography and Historiophoty." *American Historical Review* 93 (December 1988): 1193–1199.

White, Jan V. *Using Charts and Graphs: 1000 Ideas for Visual Persuasion*. New York: Bowker, 1984.

Wood, Denis. *The Power of Maps*. New York: Guilford Press, 1992.

Index

About the Author

David J. Staley is an historian and futurist who teaches at Heidelberg College in Tiffin, Ohio.